COUNTRIES OF THE WORLD

AUSTRALIA

ABDO
Publishing Company

AUSTRALIA

by Susan Hamen

Content Consultant
Alan C. Tidwell
Director of the Center for Australian and New Zealand Studies
Georgetown University

CREDITS

Published by ABDO Publishing Company, PO Box 398166, Minneapolis, MN 55439.
Copyright © 2013 by Abdo Consulting Group, Inc. International copyrights reserved
in all countries. No part of this book may be reproduced in any form without written
permission from the publisher. The Essential Library™ is a trademark and logo of ABDO
Publishing Company.

Printed in the United States of America,
North Mankato, Minnesota
092012
012013

 THIS BOOK CONTAINS AT LEAST 10% RECYCLED MATERIALS.

Editor: Arnold Ringstad
Series Designer: Emily Love

About the Author: Susan E. Hamen is a full-time editor and freelance writer who finds
her most rewarding career experiences to be writing children's books. Hamen lives in
Minnesota with her husband and two children. She would like to thank Dave Finlayson and
Anna Taff-Burton for sharing their invaluable knowledge and experiences of Australia.

Cataloging-in-Publication Data

Hamen, Susan E.
 Australia / Susan E. Hamen.
   p. cm. -- (Countries of the world)
Includes bibliographical references and index.
ISBN 978-1-61783-626-8
1. Australia--Juvenile literature.   1. Title.
994--dc22

                                          2012946072

Cover: The Sydney Opera House

TABLE OF CONTENTS

CHAPTER 1

A VISIT TO AUSTRALIA

As the ferry draws up toward Sydney's Circular Quay after your morning of harbor hopping, the sight of the world-famous Sydney Opera House takes your breath away. The iconic building, with its billowing sail roof and beautiful harbor view, is set against a backdrop of the city's skyscrapers, wharfs, and historic buildings. Sydney, the capital of New South Wales, Australia, is a sight to behold.

Just to the right of the opera house, across Sydney Cove, stretches the famous Sydney Harbour Bridge, lovingly dubbed "The Coathanger" due to its shape. You are still contemplating a climb to the top of the structure, which reaches 439 feet (134 m) above sea level and connects Sydney's central business district to the commercial and residential areas of the North

The name *Australia* is derived from the Latin *australis*, meaning "southern."

The Sydney Harbour Bridge opened in 1932.

SYDNEY OPERA HOUSE

The Sydney Opera House boasts the distinction of being the most photographed landmark in Australia. It is among the most famous buildings of the twentieth century, as well as one of the most prestigious performing arts venues in the world. This unique structure sits on Bennelong Point in Sydney Harbour and stands across Sydney Cove from the famous Sydney Harbour Bridge. The opera house's curious design was the result of a competition launched in 1956. The final design, submitted by Danish architect Jørn Utzon, was selected from 233 entries from 28 different countries. Construction began in March 1959, and the project was completed in 1973 at a cost of $AU 102 million, well above the estimated budget of $AU 7 million.[1] On June 28, 2007, the Sydney Opera House was made a United Nations Educational, Scientific, and Cultural Organization (UNESCO) World Heritage Site.

Shore. Perhaps you will make the ascent after some more sightseeing.

After disembarking in Sydney Harbour, you cross George Street and make your way toward the Rocks, Sydney's historic district. It consists of narrow streets and centuries-old stone buildings recently restored to their former glory. Once a den of thieves, pickpockets, and gangs, the area is now home to boutiques, art dealers, cafés, and other quaint shops. You peruse the Rocks Market, leisurely strolling past stalls selling food, art, flowers, original photography, handmade jewelry and accessories, and various other interesting items. Sydneysiders, or residents of Sydney, greet you with a smile and a "G'day!" as you pass by. The smell of fish and chips wafts in the air and entices you to an early lunch.

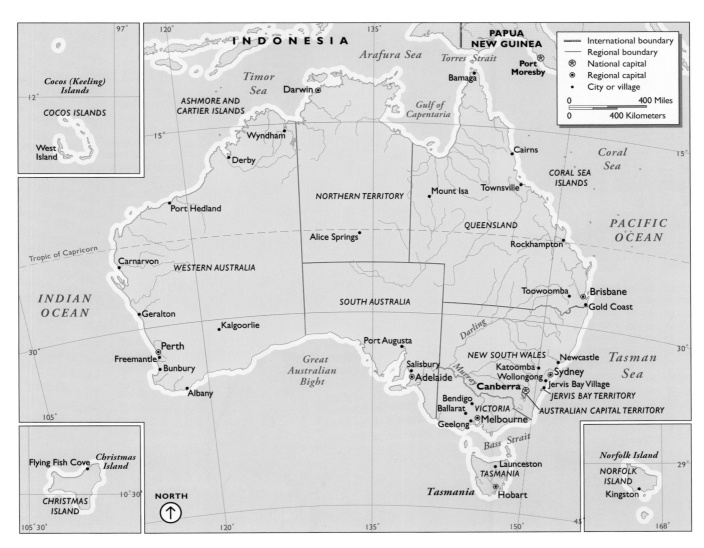

Political Boundaries of Australia

Cocos (Keeling) Islands
COCOS ISLANDS
West Island

INDONESIA
Arafura Sea
Torres Strait
PAPUA NEW GUINEA
Port Moresby
Bamaga

Timor Sea
ASHMORE AND CARTIER ISLANDS
Darwin
Gulf of Capentaria

Wyndham
Derby

Cairns
Coral Sea

NORTHERN TERRITORY
Mount Isa
Townsville
CORAL SEA ISLANDS

Port Hedland
QUEENSLAND
PACIFIC OCEAN

Tropic of Capricorn
Alice Springs
Rockhampton

Carnarvon
WESTERN AUSTRALIA
INDIAN OCEAN
SOUTH AUSTRALIA

Geralton
Kalgoorlie
Toowoomba
Brisbane
Gold Coast

Darling
Port Augusta

Perth
Freemantle
Bunbury
NEW SOUTH WALES
Newcastle
Tasman Sea
Great Australian Bight
Salisbury
Katoomba
Wollongong
Sydney
Murray
Adelaide
Jervis Bay Village
JERVIS BAY TERRITORY
Canberra
Albany

Bendigo
Ballarat
VICTORIA
AUSTRALIAN CAPITAL TERRITORY
Geelong
Melbourne

Bass Strait

Flying Fish Cove
Christmas Island
Launceston
TASMANIA
Norfolk Island
NORFOLK ISLAND
Kingston

CHRISTMAS ISLAND
NORTH
Tasmania
Hobart

Following your meal, you walk a short distance to Darling Harbour. The Sydney Aquarium awaits you. You investigate jellyfish, stingrays, sharks, and starfish up close behind the aquarium glass as you make your way through the transparent underwater tunnels. You excitedly anticipate the next leg of your journey through Australia, up the coast toward Cairns where the Great Barrier Reef awaits. You cannot wait to try your hand at snorkeling, swimming with dolphins, deep-sea fishing, and exploring the world-renowned beaches of the Gold Coast near Brisbane.

A CITY OF SPORT

In the year 2000, Sydney was host to the Summer Olympic Games. The games had previously been hosted in Australia in 1956 in Melbourne. Sydney was also the venue for the British Empire Games of 1938 and the 2003 Rugby World Cup.

The cheerful, laid-back locals had informed you that a trip to Sydney would not be complete without a stop at the Sydney Tower, so you are sure to add it to your itinerary. This 1,014-foot (309 m) tower, opened to the public in 1981, is among the tallest structures in the Southern Hemisphere. The view from its observatory deck stretches for miles in every direction, and you see your first glimpse of the Blue Mountains

Sydney Tower, one of the tallest structures in the Southern Hemisphere, stands beside Darling Harbour.

in the distance. Tomorrow's train ride will take you up to the town of Katoomba in the Blue Mountains, where you anticipate a tranquil hike to the mountains' scenic vista. The Three Sisters, a famous rock formation, is an easy walk from the streets of the town, and you are looking forward to some breathtaking photo opportunities.

Making your way back to Darling Harbour later in the afternoon, you are treated to a beautiful Australian sight as you spot a pod of dolphins frolicking in the waters of the harbor. Tourists and residents point and laugh as the playful creatures breach and splash. You smile, knowing that your list of new animal sightings is growing. Just the day before, you observed bouncing kangaroos and shy koalas.

Sydney received nearly 7.6 million visitors in 2011.

Strolling toward the Royal Botanical Gardens among the throng of international tourists, Australians, and Sydneysiders, you marvel at the warm climate, the friendly people, and the amazing native animals. Australia is truly a remarkable part of the world.

A LAND OF DIVERSITY AND WONDER

Australia is a nation of humble beginnings. It was built by banished convicts who were sent off with the intention that they would never

The Royal Botanical Gardens in Sydney are nestled within the cityscape.

be seen or heard from again. Against unfavorable odds, the Land Down Under has flourished, transforming into a world contender in trade, tourism, mining, manufacturing, art, and many other arenas.

Australia has also become a melting pot of different cultures, welcoming immigrants from Europe, Asia, Africa, and the Americas. What was once a land of just two groups, indigenous Aborigines and English settlers, has now grown to include ethnic backgrounds from around the world.

Australia has one of the lowest population densities of any country in the world.

SNAPSHOT

Official name: Commonwealth of Australia

Capital city: Canberra

Form of government: federal parliamentary democracy

Title of leaders: prime minister (head of government); king or queen (head of state)

Currency: Australian dollar

Population (July 2012 est.): 22,015,576
World rank: 54

Size: 2,988,902 square miles (7,741,220 sq km)
World rank: 6

Language: English

Official religion: none

Per capita GDP (2011, US dollars): $40,800
World rank: 22

CHAPTER 2

GEOGRAPHY: THE LAND DOWN UNDER

Australia is often called the Land Down Under. The nickname refers to its location in the Southern Hemisphere, below the equator. It is also called the Last of Lands because, apart from Antarctica, it was the last continent explored by Europeans and is geographically one of the most isolated nations on Earth.

Australia has the distinction of being the only country that is also a continent. With a landmass approximately the size of the contiguous United States, Australia is a large country diverse in landforms and climates. Tropical rain forests, barren deserts, gently rolling pasture lands, and white sandy beaches are just a sampling of the vast array of geographical elements found on the smallest continent on Earth.

Australia is full of diverse landscapes, including this rocky and tree-lined coast at Roebuck Bay in Western Australia.

AN ISOLATED COUNTRY

Australia is the flattest continent and the second driest continent, after Antarctica.[1] Its average elevation is approximately 900 feet (274 m), compared to the world average of 2,300 feet (700 m).[2] It lies in the Southern Hemisphere between the South Pacific Ocean and the Indian Ocean. To the northeast and northwest lie the island countries of Papua New Guinea and Indonesia. The Coral Sea and Torres Strait separate Australia from Papua New Guinea, and the Timor Sea separates it from Indonesia. Across the Tasman Sea to the southeast is New Zealand. The island of Tasmania sits 150 miles (240 km) off the southeast coast of mainland Australia, across the Bass Strait. It is one of Australia's states. Far to the south, across 1,600 miles (2,575 km) of the Indian Ocean, lies Antarctica.[3]

The sixth largest country in the world, Australia has an area of 2,988,901 square miles (7,741,220 sq km).[4] It has

ULURU

Uluru, formerly known as Ayers Rock, is a 1,142-foot (348 m) tall sandstone rock formation that rises out of the desolate desert of central Australia. The iron oxide in the sandstone makes the rock appear to glow red at dawn and sunset. Uluru, which is approximately 5.8 miles (9.4 km) in circumference, is sacred to the Anangu Aboriginal people. It is also a World Heritage Site.

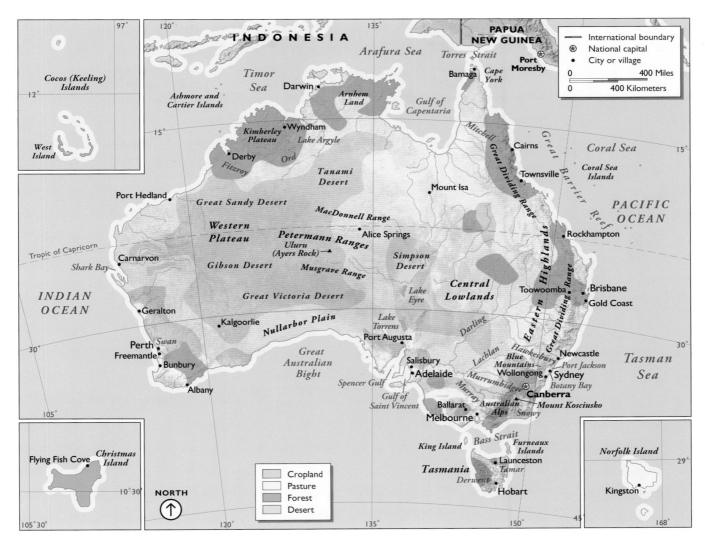

INDONESIA

Arafura Sea

Torres Strait

PAPUA
NEW GUINEA

Timor
Sea

Ashmore and
Cartier Islands

Darwin

Arnhem
Land

Gulf of
Capentaria

Bamaga

Cape
York

Port
Moresby

Cocos (Keeling)
Islands

West
Island

Kimberley
Plateau

Wyndham

Lake Argyle

Mitchell

Great Barrier Reef

Coral Sea

Cairns

Derby

Ord

Fitzroy

Tanami
Desert

Mount Isa

Townsville

Coral Sea
Islands

PACIFIC
OCEAN

Port Hedland

Great Sandy Desert

MacDonnell Range

Great Dividing Range

Rockhampton

Western
Plateau

Petermann Ranges

Alice Springs

Tropic of Capricorn

Carnarvon

Uluru
(Ayers Rock)

Simpson
Desert

Eastern Highlands

Shark Bay

Gibson Desert

Musgrave Range

Great Victoria Desert

Lake
Eyre

Central
Lowlands

Toowoomba

Great Dividing Range

Brisbane

INDIAN
OCEAN

Geralton

Kalgoorlie

Nullarbor Plain

Lake
Torrens

Darling

Gold Coast

Perth

Swan

Freemantle

Port Augusta

Bunbury

Great
Australian
Bight

Salisbury

Adelaide

Lachlan

Blue
Mountains

Murrumbidgee

Hawkesbury

Newcastle

Port Jackson

Wollongong

Sydney

Botany Bay

Tasman
Sea

Albany

Spencer Gulf

Gulf of
Saint Vincent

Ballarat

Murray

Australian
Alps

Snowy

Canberra

Mount Kosciusko

Melbourne

Bass Strait

King Island

Furneaux
Islands

Norfolk Island

Flying Fish Cove

Christmas
Island

Launceston

Tamar

Tasmania

Derwent

Kingston

NORTH

Hobart

International boundary
National capital
City or village

0   400 Miles
0   400 Kilometers

Cropland
Pasture
Forest
Desert

Geography of Australia

AVERAGE TEMPERATURE AND PRECIPITATION

Region (City)	Average January Temperature Minimum/Maximum	Average July Temperature Minimum/Maximum	Average Precipitation January/July
Australian Capital Territory (Canberra)	55/82°F (12/27°C)	32/52°F (0/11°C)	2.3/1.6 inches (5.8/4.1 cm)
New South Wales (Sydney)	65/69°F (18/26°C)	44/62°F (6/16°C)	4/2.5 inches (10.2/6.4 cm)
South Australia (Adelaide)	60/82°F (15/27°C)	44/59°F (6/15°C)	0.7/2.5 inches (1.8/6.4 cm)
Tasmania (Hobart)	53/71°F (11/21°C)	40/52°F (4/11°C)	1.9/2.1 inches (4.8/5.3 cm)
Victoria (Melbourne)	56/79°F (13/26°C)	41/55°F (5/12°C)	1.8/1.5 inches (4.6/3.8 cm)
Western Australia (Perth)	62/89°F (16/31°C)	46/64°F (7/17°C)	0.3/6.4 inches (0.8/16.3 cm)[6]

approximately 23,000 miles (37,000 km) of shoreline.[5] The Southern Hemisphere experiences seasons at the opposite time to those in the Northern Hemisphere. Summertime in the United States is

Australia's winter, and wintertime in the United States brings Australia's summer season.

CLIMATE REGIONS

The center of the country is predominantly composed of arid desert. More than two-thirds of the country's landmass receives less than 20 inches (51 cm) of precipitation annually.[7] The Australian Alps, along with parts of Tasmania, are the only regions in Australia that regularly receive snow.

The northern half of Australia lies in the tropical zone. The far north experiences a monsoon season from November to April and a dry season from May to October. Southern Australia has a temperate climate with warm summers and cool, wet winters.

Further inland, toward the massive arid landscape of central Australia, temperatures can reach 118 degrees Fahrenheit (43°C) or higher.[8] Droughts are common in Australia and some can last several years. Bush fires and water shortages are common problems in the nation's drier regions.

LAND FEATURES

Australia is divided into three major land regions: the Eastern Highlands, the Central Lowlands, and the Western Plateau. The Eastern Highlands, also called the Great Dividing Range, run down the coast and stretch more than 2,200 miles (3,540 km) from Cape York in northern Queensland down to southern Tasmania. This region has low plains, rocky cliffs, and sandy beaches, and it is the most populated area of the country. Its western edge consists of high plateaus, hills, and low mountains. The Great Dividing Range includes both the Blue Mountains and the Australian Alps. The Alps are home to Mount Kosciuszko, the country's highest point at 7,310 feet (2,229 m).[9] The Eastern Highlands are home to the country's best farmland.

THE TWELVE APOSTLES

Just off the shore of the Port Campbell National Park in Victoria, limestone pillars rise up to 150 feet (45 m) from the Southern Ocean. These picturesque rock formations, formed by erosion, are a popular tourist destination. Despite the name, there were never more than nine of them. Sightseers can view this iconic Australian landmark from the Great Ocean Road, a 151-mile (243 km) road that winds along the southeast coast of Victoria.

To the west, beyond the Great Dividing Range, lie the Central Lowlands, a large, flat area of dry soil, tough grass, and scrubby shrubs. Lake Eyre, Australia's lowest point at 53 feet (16 m) below sea level, is found in the Lowlands. The lake is usually completely dry and covered in a white, salty crust. Dry riverbeds in the Lowlands fill with water when enough rain falls. The Simpson Desert covers the western area of

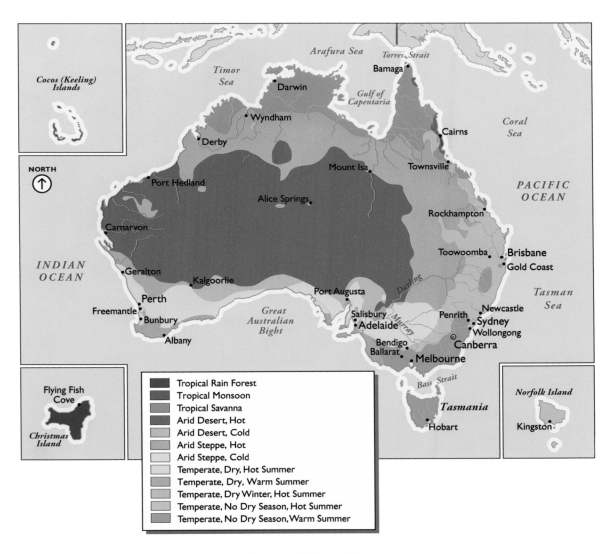

Cocos (Keeling)
Islands

Arafura Sea

Torres Strait

Timor
Sea

Bamaga

Darwin

Gulf of
Capentaria

Wyndham

Coral
Sea

Derby

Cairns

NORTH
↑

Townsville

PACIFIC
OCEAN

Mount Isa

Port Hedland

Alice Springs

Carnarvon

Rockhampton

INDIAN
OCEAN

Geralton

Toowoomba   Brisbane

Kalgoorlie

Gold Coast

Port Augusta

Darling

Tasman
Sea

Perth

Great
Australian
Bight

Salisbury
Adelaide

Penrith   Newcastle
Murray   Sydney
          Wollongong

Freemantle

Bunbury

Albany

Bendigo
Ballarat

Canberra

Melbourne

Flying Fish
Cove

Bass Strait

Norfolk Island

Tasmania

Christmas
Island

Hobart

Kingston

Tropical Rain Forest
Tropical Monsoon
Tropical Savanna
Arid Desert, Hot
Arid Desert, Cold
Arid Steppe, Hot
Arid Steppe, Cold
Temperate, Dry, Hot Summer
Temperate, Dry, Warm Summer
Temperate, Dry Winter, Hot Summer
Temperate, No Dry Season, Hot Summer
Temperate, No Dry Season, Warm Summer

Climate of Australia

the Lowlands in the center of the country. In the southern part of the Lowlands, ranchers raise cattle and sheep.

The Western Plateau covers two-thirds of Australia's land. This area is mostly flat, with the exception of the MacDonnell, Musgrave, and Petermann mountain ranges. Although rain does fall in the far north and southwest, most of the region consists of large deserts, including the Gibson, Great Sandy, Great Victoria, and Tanami deserts. The Nullarbor Plain (Latin for "no tree") runs along the southern coast of the Western Plateau, and as its name implies, virtually no trees grow there. In the middle of the plateau stands a massive rock formation, Uluru, which is a sacred site for Aborigines. Bungle Bungles, a small range of hills in this region, features colorful sandstone rock carved into strange shapes by the wind. Although the term "outback" can refer to any inland area remote from population centers, generally the Outback refers to the hot, dry center of Australia's Western Plateau.

WATERWAYS

Australia has very few rivers or lakes. In the interior of the country, lake beds remain dry the majority of the year, holding water only after heavy rains. Likewise, many inland rivers are dry throughout the year until hard rains come. The Murray-Darling river system, the largest in the country, is located in the southeastern portion of Australia. The Murray River itself

Australia's interior regions are usually dry.

AUSTRALIA'S BIG CITIES

The vast majority of Australia's population is divided among its five largest cities: Sydney, Melbourne, Brisbane, Perth, and Adelaide. All are coastal cities. After Sydney, Melbourne is the nation's second-largest city. It is considered to be the cultural capital of the country and is the birthplace of the nation's film industry, as well as a major center for traditional and contemporary Australian music.

Brisbane, the most populous city in Queensland, has the largest economy of any city between Sydney and Singapore. It is home to petroleum refining, metalworking, paper milling, financial services, administrative jobs, and tourist destinations.

Perth, located on Australia's west coast, has a Mediterranean climate. On hot summer afternoons, a sea breeze dubbed "The Fremantle Doctor" blows from the southwest and offers relief from the hot winds that descend from the northeast. The Western Australian Museum, which offers an extensive display of Aboriginal artifacts, is located in Perth.

Adelaide, the capital of South Australia, is a city of more than 1 million people. It possesses good farmland and nearby mineral deposits, and its central location has allowed it to easily ship its goods throughout Australia.

is approximately 1,550 miles (2,500 km) long.[10] The Snowy River starts in the Australian Alps in New South Wales and runs to the ocean, while the Murrumbidgee River also originates in the Alps but is a tributary of the Murray River. Other major river systems include the Fitzroy River in Queensland, the Ord and Swan Rivers in Western Australia, the Derwent and Tamar Rivers in Tasmania, and the Hawkesbury River in New South Wales.

STATES AND TERRITORIES

Australia is divided into six states and two mainland territories. The states include Western Australia,

Uluru, a sacred rock formation, glows red
at sunset.

Queensland, South Australia, New South Wales, Victoria, and Tasmania.
The mainland territories are the Northern Territory and the Australian
Capital Territory. The latter consists of Canberra, the nation's capital, and
is totally surrounded by New South Wales.

The Ashmore and Cartier Islands, the Heard and McDonald Islands,
the Coral Sea Islands, and the Australian Antarctic Territory are all external
territories of Australia, but none are populated. Australia also claims
Christmas Island, Norfolk Island, and the Cocos (Keeling) Islands as external
territories. They have a combined population of nearly 4,000 people.[11]

CHAPTER 3

ANIMALS AND NATURE: A UNIQUE ASSORTMENT

Among Australia's most remarkable features is its collection of truly unique animals. Thoughts of the Land Down Under usually conjure images of bounding kangaroos and tree-dwelling koalas, both of which are marsupials native to Australia. But these are only two of the country's many fascinating creatures.

Australia was once part of a large landmass that included Africa, Madagascar, India, Antarctica, New Zealand, and South America. However, over time, these continents broke apart, taking the local animals with them. Australia's separation and subsequent isolation caused its plants and animals to evolve differently from those in the rest of the world.

Kangaroos are just one of the many unique animals of Australia.

INTRIGUING MARSUPIALS

Early European explorers of Australia were likely surprised at their first glimpses of kangaroos, hopping animals with long hind legs and short forelegs unlike anything seen in Europe. The kangaroo is one of approximately 200 species of marsupials found almost exclusively in Australia.[1] Marsupials are the dominant mammals in Australia.

Most marsupials can be distinguished by the special flap of skin or pouch found on the females. Offspring have an extremely short gestation period and are born underdeveloped. The newborn marsupial is blind, lacks fur, and has hind limbs that are not fully formed. However, the helpless newborn is able to climb its way into the pouch of its mother. Here, it attaches itself to her teat, feeding and continuing to develop until it is ready for the outside world.

Large kangaroos can cover more than 30 feet (9 m) in one leap.

The largest living marsupials are kangaroos. There are several distinct species, including the red kangaroo and eastern gray kangaroo. They can reach heights of over 6.6 feet (2 m) and can weigh up to 200 pounds (90 kg). The smallest kangaroo is called a rat kangaroo. This small animal runs rather than hops, and it is only approximately one foot (30 cm) long. Kangaroos spend most of their days resting and seeking shade. They are mostly active at night, grazing on grasses or leaves.

The koala is another species commonly associated with Australia. These furry, gray marsupials with dark noses have long, hook-like limbs

that facilitate hanging and sleeping in trees. A koala eats several pounds of eucalyptus leaves daily. Males, averaging approximately twice the size of females, can weigh 30 pounds (13.5 kg) and reach 2.7 feet (82 cm) in length. Baby koalas, called joeys, stay in their mother's pouch for six to seven months and then remain with her for another year.

The possum, another marsupial, is related to and named after the opossum of North America. These tree-dwelling animals can reach 37 inches (95 cm) in length. While some species of possum are endangered and protected, the common brush-tailed possum is actually considered a pest, and steps have been taken to reduce its population. Possums, often found in the suburbs, are among the most commonly encountered animals for many Australians.

DANGEROUS WILDLIFE

Australia is home to a great number of creatures that are deadly to humans as well as to other animals. Crocodiles are Australia's largest living reptiles and reside only in the north. Saltwater crocodiles, the largest species, can grow up to 23 feet (7 m) in length and weigh more than 2,200 pounds (1,000 kg). Despite their name, they can also be found in freshwater rivers and wetlands. In addition to eating fish, birds, wallabies, and dingoes, these crocodiles will attack and kill humans who get too close.

Australia is home to many of the world's deadliest snakes. The taipan and inland taipan are extremely venomous. The venom of the inland taipan is much more potent than the venom of South Asia's notorious king cobra; a single bite contains enough venom to kill

Crocodiles eat many kinds of animals.

100 adult humans.[2] Other highly venomous snakes in Australia include the eastern tiger snake and the death adder.

While Australia is home to a host of the world's deadliest snakes, fatality rates from snakebite are low. On average, fewer than five people die each year from venomous snakebites.[3] In comparison, an average of 46,000 people die each year in India from snakebites.[4]

Snakes are not the only venomous creatures in Australia. The sea wasp, also known as the box jellyfish, is among the most venomous animals on Earth. This sea creature has a square-shaped, pale blue, transparent body with many long tentacles. It is very difficult to see in the water. The tentacles leave horribly painful stings wherever they contact human skin, and the venom can kill a human in less than four minutes. The blue-ringed octopus is yet another extremely venomous animal found in Australian waters.

MONOTREMES

Mammals that lay eggs are called monotremes and are found only in Australia and New Guinea. There are only two species of monotremes in the world: the platypus and the echidna.

The platypus stumped early explorers. They believed the animal to be a mammal with the bill of a duck sewn onto the mouth. Platypuses are covered in brown fur and have a long bill, webbed feet with claws, and a flat tail that acts as a rudder as the creature swims. They eat worms and small crustaceans. Males have a spur above each ankle connected to a venom gland. If the spur penetrates the skin of a predator, the sting is very painful. Biologists believe the venom is used as an offensive weapon during the competitive mating season, rather than simply as a defensive weapon.

Echidnas look a bit like large hedgehogs, with long spines and fur. Their diet consists of ants, termites, and other insects. Echidnas eat by shooting their long tongue from their elongated, tubelike snout.

INTRODUCED ANIMALS

Dingoes are wild dogs that were most likely introduced to Australia by seafarers a few thousand years ago. They are carnivores and often prey upon sheep, small cattle, rabbits, and occasionally kangaroos.

When Europeans came to settle in Australia, they brought with them animals from their homelands. Livestock such as cattle, sheep, pigs, donkeys, and goats were introduced to Australia, as were rabbits, foxes, deer, domestic dogs, and cats. Rabbits and feral cats have reached pest proportions, with cats killing small animals and birds.

A few thousand cane toads were introduced in Queensland in 1935 by the Australian government in an attempt to control the population of beetles in sugarcane fields. However, these toads proved poisonous to other animals and have very few predators. They quickly multiplied and spread across Australia. Population estimates are now approximately 200 million.[5]

BIRDS AND REPTILES

Australia has hundreds of different species of birds. The emu, a large flightless bird, can be found throughout much of the Australian mainland. This bird, which can reach 6.5 feet (2 m) tall, has large three-toed feet and shaggy feathers. In the early twentieth century, emus were hunted because they destroyed farmers' wheat fields. Today, they are farmed in Australia for their low-cholesterol meat, eggs, oil, feathers, and leather.

The cassowary, another flightless bird, is the world's second-heaviest bird after the ostrich. Cassowaries live in the tropical rain forests of northeastern Queensland and New Guinea and can grow to heights of 6.5 feet (2 m). This blue-headed bird has a casque, which is a bony, helmetlike structure on the top of its head.

Australia's coastal regions, tropical forests, and other diverse habitats are alive with colorful birds including cockatoos, lorikeets, and dozens of species of parrots. Brush turkeys, crested pigeons, cranes, pelicans, wedge-tailed eagles, and black and chestnut colored shelducks are just a few of the other bird species found in Australia. On the southern coast of the mainland, the little penguin, the smallest penguin species, lives and breeds.

Cassowaries are large, flightless birds. Males show off their brightly colored heads and necks to attract mates.

One of the most significant animals in Australian culture is the goanna. This lizard, named after the iguana of South America, is a component of the folklore of both the Aboriginal people and European settlers. It is frequently seen in indigenous artwork and was a food source for Aborigines. Settlers developed urban legends about the goanna, exaggerating its ferociousness.

THE GREAT BARRIER REEF

The Great Barrier Reef has been described as the largest structure built by living organisms. It consists of a series of reefs that run along the northeast coast of Australia in the waters of the Coral Sea. These reefs are formed from the skeletons of living marine organisms. They are cemented together by a hard substance called coralline, which is produced by algae. In 1981, the Great Barrier Reef was designated as a UNESCO World Heritage Site.

British explorer James Cook ran his ship aground on the Great Barrier Reef in 1770.

The reef is home to more than 1,500 species of fish and 300 species of hard coral.[6] Brightly colored clownfish, angelfish, surgeonfish, blue tangs, triggerfish, and other exotic saltwater fish dart around coral and sponges as sea anemones, jellyfish, manta rays, giant clams, lobsters, prawns, crabs, sea snails, and other sea creatures swim and crawl through the blue waters of the reef. Groupers

The Great Barrier Reef

and sharks, the large predators in the reef, lurk in the water looking for prey.

Other marine creatures living in the coastal waters include humpback whales, sea turtles, dolphins, and dugongs, which are marine mammals similar to manatees.

FLORA

Australia's plant life features many species unique to the region. But the arrival of Europeans to the continent resulted in significant changes. Much of the native vegetation was stripped away, and nonnative plants and crops were introduced. Additionally, with the introduction of millions of grazing livestock such as sheep and cattle, native vegetation was strained, occasionally to the point of extinction.

Australian vegetation is dominated by two groups of plants, eucalyptus and acacias. Eucalyptus trees, or gum trees as Australians know them, grow as tall as 328 feet (100 m). Other species of eucalyptus grow only to shrub height and are called mallee. They can be found in rain forests, in the Snowy Mountains, and even on the desert fringes. The leaves secrete a fragrant, flammable oil, yet the thick bark protects the gum tree during bushfires. The acacia, or wattle, is a genus of blossoming plants with either feathery leaves or spine-like structures in place

Eucalyptus trees are among the tallest flowering plants in the world.

THE AMAZING EUCALYPTUS TREE

Koalas are not the only creatures that rely upon the eucalyptus tree. Termites hollow out the trees, turning the wood into a pulp they feed upon and use for their young. Butterfly larvae and caterpillars also eat the leaves of the eucalyptus tree. Additionally, many of Australia's birds and mammals make their homes in these trees. Humans have also discovered valuable uses for this indigenous tree. Fragrant eucalyptus oils are used in perfumes, cold medications, throat lozenges, and chest rubs.

of leaves. The acacia is depicted on Australia's coat of arms.

In the far north, dense tropical rain forests and mangrove swamps grow in the hot and humid weather. In drier regions, scrublands with small shrubs and bushes manage to survive in arid grasslands. Further into the Outback, plant life becomes sparse. There, plant life consists mainly of desert wildflowers, such as the everlasting daisy, that are tolerant of the low moisture conditions.

ENVIRONMENTAL THREATS

Australia's incredible collection of plant and animal life is under threat from an assortment of environmental challenges. In the past, extinctions were caused by species introduced to Australia by newcomers. This is still a factor today, with many new pests or diseases being introduced to Australia each year. Other major threats to Australia's environment include deforestation, overfishing, and pollution.

Cutting down forests can raise the amount of salt dissolved in soil. This reduces water quality downstream from the impacted area, harming agriculture. Studies have estimated that the resulting annual cost of this damage is approximately $AU 1 billion.[7]

The slow reproduction rates of some species of fish, along with overly concentrated fishing efforts, have dangerously reduced the stocks of many Australian fish species. Pollution in the form of fertilizer runoff from farms near the coasts also damages the habitats of fish and other animals living off Australia's shores.

ENDANGERED SPECIES IN AUSTRALIA

According to the International Union for Conservation of Nature (IUCN), Australia is home to the following numbers of species that are categorized by the organization as Critically Endangered, Endangered, or Vulnerable:

Mammals	55
Birds	52
Reptiles	43
Amphibians	47
Fishes	103
Mollusks	168
Other Invertebrates	314
Plants	67
Total	849[8]

However, the people of Australia have taken steps to protect their environment. The federal government and the state and territorial governments have established more than 500 national parks, covering nearly 4 percent of the nation's enormous land area. Another 6 percent is designated as protected, meaning that approximately a tenth of Australia has been set aside for plant and animal life.[9] In these areas, commercial activities such as farming and fishing are not allowed, and all activity is carefully observed and managed.

Deforestation is one of many threats to Australia's natural environment.

CHAPTER 4

HISTORY: HUMBLE BEGINNINGS

The earliest humans on the Australian continent were Aborigines. They were given this name by the European explorers who came thousands of years later. It is an English word with Latin roots meaning "from the beginning." Scientists estimate Australian Aborigines came to the continent in approximately 50,000 BCE, traveling via land bridges or short sea crossings from South or Southeast Asia at a time when the ocean levels were lower than they are now.

Tribes of Aborigines spread out across the continent and Tasmania, forming clans composed of several families. They developed their own languages, religions, and customs. For food, they hunted animals such as kangaroos, reptiles, birds, fish, and insects, and gathered roots, fruits, tubers, and other edible plants. Clans were nomadic, moving around when food became scarce rather than staying in one place.

Aborigine men use traditional methods to make fire.

Aborigines developed tools and weapons that enabled them to hunt. Boomerangs, woven nets, spears, and axes allowed them to hunt kangaroos and trap wallabies and other small animals. They also utilized sharpened sticks to dig up edible roots. When Aborigines brought dingoes with them to Australia, they trained the wild dogs to assist in hunting.

Early Aborigines who came to Australia used rafts or canoes to traverse the open ocean.

Aboriginal clans had no written history. Instead, they passed on stories through oral stories, songs, and art. Their rock drawings can still be seen in the Outback. Some of their stories tell of the creation of the Aborigines in what is called the Dreamtime. During this time, it is said, Aboriginal ancestors and spirits lived together.

When Europeans made their way to Australia, the Aborigines living on the continent were divided into approximately 500 tribes and spoke nearly 260 different languages.[1]

EUROPEANS SET FOOT ONTO AUSTRALIA

Long before Europeans first saw Australia, many of them believed there must be a landmass south of Asia. This unknown continent was called Terra Australis Incognita, which means "unknown land in the south." Their hunch was correct.

Dutch explorers were responsible for much of the early exploration of Australia. In 1605, Dutch navigator Willem Janszoon sailed from the Dutch East Indies (modern Indonesia) in search of New Guinea. He landed on Australia in 1606 at what is now Cape York Peninsula in the Torres Strait. Dutch explorers Dirck Hartog and Jan Carstensz landed on the continent in 1616 and 1623, respectively. A few decades later, in 1642, Abel Tasman discovered the island south of mainland Australia, now called Tasmania in his honor. William Dampier, an Englishman, landed on the continent in 1688. He returned a decade later to further explore the continent the Dutch had named New Holland.

AUSTRALIA BECOMES A PENAL COLONY

On April 20, 1770, Captain James Cook of Britain's Royal Navy landed his ship *Endeavour* south of what would become the city of Sydney. He claimed the land in the name of King George III of Great Britain. He named the eastern coast of Australia New South Wales. Sir Joseph Banks, a botanist who sailed with Cook and his crew, was stunned by the Australian plant life at the bay where the ship landed. He named the area Botany Bay.

In 1787, Britain sent a fleet of ships back to Australia. But the ships transported neither adventurers nor scientists. Instead, the first fleet of ships carried prisoners Britain wanted to banish to a far-off land, along with their guards.

THE FIRST FLEET

The First Fleet ships carried 759 convicts and 246 officers, marines, ship crew, and their families.[3]
The fleet was comprised of six convict ships, three supply ships, and two naval war ships.

The ships were named:

Convict ships: *Alexander, Charlotte, Lady Penrhyn, Friendship, Prince of Wales,* and *Scarborough*
Supply ships: *Fishburn, Borrowdale,* and *Golden Grove*
War ships: H.M.S. *Sirius* and H.M.S. *Supply*

At the time, Britain had overflowing prisons. To remedy this, Britain had been expelling prisoners to British plantations in America, Africa, Asia, and the West Indies. However, by the late 1780s, the United States had won its independence and no longer tolerated being, as one colonist described it, "the very common sewer and dung yard to Britain."[2]

The first group of 11 ships carrying prisoners and supplies, called the First Fleet, left England on May 13, 1787. Captain Arthur Phillip was in command. The group included more than 750 convicts, nearly 200 of them women. They arrived at Botany Bay in late January of the following year but found the area to have poor soil and little water. Phillip commanded the fleet to sail northward a few miles in search of better land. They landed at

A depiction of Captain Arthur Phillip claiming Australia for England in 1788.

Port Jackson, hoisting the British flag and establishing their colony on January 26, 1788, in Sydney Cove. This was the first European settlement in Australia, and this day is celebrated as Australia Day, much as July 4 is celebrated as Independence Day in the United States. The day is sometimes called Invasion Day by Aboriginal Australians.

MORE MIGRATE TO AUSTRALIA

Phillip served as the colony's first governor from 1788 to 1792. More colonies were established as more than 160,000 men, women, and children prisoners were sent to Australia over the course of 80 years.[4] They learned to clear and farm the land, and they built homes and buildings. Prisoners who demonstrated good behavior were sometimes set free after serving only half of their original sentences. These freed prisoners were called emancipists. They became part of a society that was growing to include soldiers, government officials, and an influx of wealthy people who were enticed by new opportunities. Skilled workers from Ireland and Britain also embarked on the lengthy sea voyage to start new lives in Australia. Emancipists were given government-owned plots of land they could farm, and many raised sheep and exported wool back to Britain.

Settlements continued to form, both free and penal. Penal stations developed at Newcastle in 1804 and Moreton Bay in 1824. Van Diemen's Land, the island southeast of the Australian mainland, became the colony of Tasmania in 1825. In 1827, a permanent settlement began at Albany in Western Australia. Two years later, a free settlement began on the site of modern day Perth. Settlements in the tropical north were less successful and were not established until the 1860s.

The rapid increase in settlements led to conflict with Australia's native people. The indigenous Aborigines were pushed off their homelands. Settlers moved into areas and took over land for grazing sheep and cattle. These "squatters," as they were called, met resistance from the Aborigines, who killed livestock and attacked homes. The squatters responded by forming armed parties that massacred groups of Aborigines. The natives' spears and shields were no match for the Europeans' firearms. Thousands of Aborigines eventually died from both armed conflict and diseases brought to Australia by settlers.

EXPLORING AUSTRALIA

From 1801 to 1803, British navigator Matthew Flinders sailed around the entire continent of Australia, discovering for the first time that Australia was one large land mass not connected to another continent. Exploration and charting of the region continued as settlers began to spread into other areas of the continent. In 1829, Royal Navy Captain Charles Fremantle landed on the southwest coast, claiming it in the name of King George IV. That same year, British explorer Charles Sturt surveyed the area of southern Australia close to modern-day Adelaide, discovering the Murray River and the extensive land that lay to the south of it. The land was ideal for livestock grazing.

From 1860 to 1861, Robert Burke and William Wills, leading a group of 18 men, crossed the continent from south to north, becoming the first non-Aboriginal people to traverse the continent. They died of starvation on their return trip.

GOLD IS DISCOVERED

In 1851, gold was discovered in the Ballarat and Bendigo regions of Victoria. Droves of miners made their way to Melbourne, aiming to strike it rich by digging for gold. Thousands of people from overseas left their jobs and homes to prospect for gold in Australia. The gold rush vastly increased the population of Europeans in the country. In 1851, it was approximately 430,000. Twenty years later, it had increased to approximately 1.7 million.[5]

Chinese also came by the thousands during the gold rush. They were met with hostility from European diggers, who attempted to drive them off. The Chinese were willing to work for less money, causing many to fear that this would drive wages down for everyone. While Irish, British, and other European diggers were accepted, animosity toward the Chinese workers continued to grow. Deadly riots broke out in some gold fields. Eventually, New South Wales restricted Chinese immigration, and Victoria enacted a tax on Chinese immigrants entering the colony.

One of the largest finds in the gold rush was the 630-pound (286 kg) Holterman Nugget.

In the midst of the gold rush, some colonial miners in Victoria protested taxes levied against them by the British authorities. This protest grew into an organized rebellion, culminating in December

The Australian gold rush spurred an increase in population and the desire for independence from Britain.

1854 in the Battle of Eureka Stockade, an armed conflict resulting in the deaths of 22 miners. This struggle for rights is an early example of Australia's efforts toward independence.

A NEW NATION

Around the time gold was discovered, the United Kingdom stopped sending its convicts to Australia's eastern colonies. But the nation that was thousands of miles from Australia was still ruling the colonies. Settlers were eager for self-government. The United Kingdom complied, granting all the colonies, with the exception of Western Australia, self-government by 1859. The United Kingdom retained control of foreign affairs, defense, and international trade.

By the 1890s, Australians wanted more control. They wanted to unite the colonies into one nation with a unified government. Conventions met in 1891 and 1897–1898 to draft a national constitution. On January 1, 1901, the Commonwealth of Australia became a nation with a new federal government. The six colonies of Australia were now states, with the exception of the Northern Territory, which remained a territory. Melbourne was named a temporary capital, but in 1908 Canberra was chosen as the site for the nation's permanent capital city. Australia was not, however, fully independent from the United Kingdom. It remained part of the British Empire. The British monarch was still the head of state in Australia.

Most women gained the right to vote in 1902, but Aborigines were still denied citizenship under the new constitution. While immigrants from Europe continued to be welcome in Australia, Asians were not. Many Australians supported a "White Australia" policy, an endeavor to keep Asian immigrants from entering Australia. The Immigration Restriction Act of 1901 was used to achieve this. Other laws were passed that actually forced nonwhite migrants out of the country.

WORLD WARS

Although thousands of miles from Europe, Australia was not insulated from World War I (1914–1918). When the United Kingdom entered the war, Australians readily enlisted to serve their empire. More than 400,000 Australians served in the only fully voluntary army in World

ANZAC DAY

During World War I, the nation's army, the Australian Imperial Force, joined forces with New Zealand's troops to form the Australian and New Zealand Army Corps (ANZAC). The combined force fought valiantly against Germany and its allies in the Middle East, France, and Belgium. In Turkey, ANZAC troops endured brutal fighting to capture the Dardanelles, a narrow strip of water on the Gallipoli Peninsula. The landing of troops at Gallipoli on April 25, 1915, is honored as the most famous engagement of the combined Australia and New Zealand Army Corps (ANZAC) during World War I. The Battle of Gallipoli became a defining moment in the histories of Australia and New Zealand. For Australia, it marked a birth of national consciousness—some say that part of the nation's identity was forged that day. Anzac Day, April 25, remains the most significant military commemoration day in Australia. It honors the men who died gallantly fighting a seemingly hopeless battle.

Australia has promised Britain 50,000 MORE MEN WILL YOU HELP US KEEP THAT PROMISE

Dyng ADELAIDE

A 1915 poster promoting Australian support of the war effort

War I. More than 60,000 of them died in the fighting.[6] When the prime minister unsuccessfully proposed mandatory military service, the country became divided in its support of the war. At war's end, more than 155,000 Australian men had been wounded or taken as prisoners of war. More than 18 percent of all who served lost their lives.[7]

When the United Kingdom entered World War II (1939–1945), Australia was called upon to fight for the British against Germany and its allies, which included Italy and Japan. The Royal Australian Air Force helped defend the United Kingdom in addition to Australia's own territory, and the Australian Navy operated in both the Mediterranean Sea and the Pacific Ocean. Ground troops fought the Germans and Italians in North Africa, Greece, and Crete.

In February 1942, Japanese forces bombed Darwin on Australia's north coast. It seemed Japan was focused on invading Australia. When Japanese troops invaded Port Moresby in New Guinea, an island just across the Torres Strait from Australia, Australia responded by sending troops to head them off. Australian troops were integral in battling the Japanese in the Pacific Islands and Southeast Asia.

THE ALLIES IN THE PACIFIC

In 1942, American General Douglas MacArthur and his troops made their base in Melbourne, which became a key staging location for retaking the Pacific following the 1941 Japanese attack on Pearl Harbor in Hawaii. Australia and the United States fought together in many Pacific campaigns, including the Battle of the Coral Sea, an important turning point in the war.

By the end of World War II, nearly 40,000 Australians had died and another 65,000 were injured.[8]

POSTWAR AUSTRALIA

After its victory in World War II, Australia had an increased sense of independence. In an effort to boost the country's population so it could compete as a modern nation, some immigration restrictions were lifted. Immigrants from all over war-torn Europe were welcomed in the 1940s. However, restrictions on Asian immigrants were still enforced. By 1960, a steady stream of European immigrants was pouring into Australia. The United Kingdom was viewed less and less as its mother country.

Furthermore, Australia had relied heavily upon the United States rather than the United Kingdom for help in fighting the Japanese. This led to increased social and political ties to the United States following World War II. In 1951, Australia signed the ANZUS Treaty, forming a military alliance with the United States and New Zealand. The treaty has become the basis upon which Australia's foreign and security policies are built. The Australian military would go on to fight alongside the United States in the Korean War (1950–1953), the Vietnam War (1955–1975), and various conflicts in the late twentieth and twenty-first centuries.

Australian soldiers man a defensive post outside Melbourne in 1942.

Australia experienced economic growth during the war. Factories churned out ammunition, airplanes, chemicals, and machine parts during the war, and suburbs began to sprout up as rural men and women moved to the cities for jobs. After the war, the export of wool and minerals helped further boost the economy. Asian nations such as Japan, Taiwan, Singapore, Indonesia, and Malaysia became important trading partners with Australia.

By 1973, the White Australia policy had been eliminated. Immigrants and refugees from Asian countries began to seek refuge from their war-torn countries in Australia. Throughout the 1970s, Australia sought to gain more independence. Although the country eventually severed some ties with the United Kingdom, the British monarch remained Australia's head of state into the twenty-first century.

Julia Gillard, who became prime minister in 2010, meets with Aboriginal elders.

CHAPTER 5

PEOPLE: A VIBRANT POPULACE

In July 2012, Australia was home to an estimated 22,015,576 people, making it the fifty-fourth most populous country in the world.[1] Though Australia is approximately the same size as the contiguous United States, the US population is more than 14 times greater than that of Australia.[2]

The vast majority of Australians live on the southeast coast. Most of Australia's population lives in just five cities: Sydney, Melbourne, Brisbane, Perth, and Adelaide, all of which are coastal cities. This is because the interior of Australia is largely desert. The Outback, occupying much of Australia's land area, is very sparsely populated.

Approximately 90 percent of Australians live in cities and towns.

Most of Australia's population is concentrated in a few urban areas, including this densely packed suburb of Hobart.

WHO LIVES IN AUSTRALIA?

When the First Fleet landed at Sydney Cove, the Australian population was entirely Aboriginal. Today, however, Aborigines comprise only 1 percent of the Australian population. People of European descent make up 92 percent, and 7 percent are Asian.[3]

The number of Australian Aborigines and Torres Strait Islanders is very small compared to Australia's total population. However, numbers have risen dramatically in the past few decades, from an estimated 115,000 in 1971 to 575,552 in 2011.[4] "Aboriginal" is a term that was given to the native peoples of Australia by Europeans. It means the native people of a country. However, there are hundreds of Aboriginal tribes, and each has its own name for itself. The Koori live in New South Wales and Victoria. The Murri dwell in southern Queensland. The Noongar are found in southern Western Australia, while the Nunga reside in South Australia. The Palawah tribe is

SLIP-SLOP-SLAP

Australians love outdoor activities, but this group of sun lovers has paid a price. Australia has the highest rate of skin cancer in the world.[5] In an effort to combat this life-threatening disease, Australia kicked off a famous campaign in the 1980s to encourage people to slip on a shirt, slop on some sunscreen, and slap on a hat. The campaign continues today.

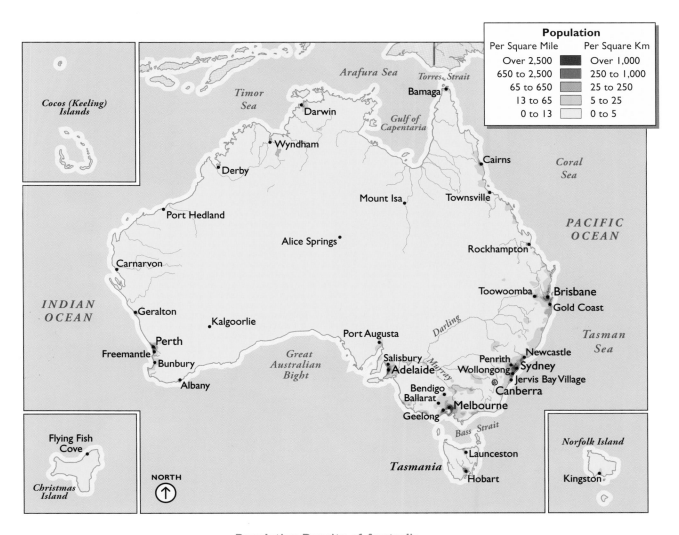

Population

Per Square Mile		Per Square Km
Over 2,500		Over 1,000
650 to 2,500		250 to 1,000
65 to 650		25 to 250
13 to 65		5 to 25
0 to 13		0 to 5

Arafura Sea

Timor Sea

Torres Strait

Bamaga

Darwin

Gulf of Capentaria

Wyndham

Cairns

Coral Sea

Derby

Mount Isa

Townsville

PACIFIC OCEAN

Port Hedland

Alice Springs

Rockhampton

Carnarvon

INDIAN OCEAN

Geralton

Kalgoorlie

Toowoomba Brisbane

Gold Coast

Perth

Port Augusta

Darling

Tasman Sea

Freemantle

Bunbury

Salisbury

Adelaide

Murray

Penrith

Wollongong

Newcastle

Sydney

Great Australian Bight

Albany

Bendigo

Ballarat

Melbourne

Geelong

Jervis Bay Village

Canberra

Cocos (Keeling) Islands

Bass Strait

Flying Fish Cove

Launceston

Norfolk Island

Christmas Island

Tasmania

Hobart

Kingston

NORTH
↑

Population Density of Australia

indigenous to Tasmania. Many more tribes are scattered across Australia.

Waves of immigrants have come to Australia since the continent was colonized in the eighteenth century. The majority of Australians are of English, Scottish, Welsh, Cornish, or Irish ancestry. Other significant groups include Bosnian, Croatian, Dutch, German, Greek, Italian, Jewish, Polish, Portuguese, Russian, Serbian, and Spanish.

In the 1970s, war in Southeast Asia prompted thousands of refugees from Vietnam, Laos, and Cambodia to flee to Australia. In recent years, Australia has experienced an influx of newcomers from Arabic-speaking Middle East countries such as Lebanon, Syria, Iraq, Jordan, and Palestine.

In 2010, the Australian Bureau of Statistics estimated that nearly 37 percent of Australian residents were born outside the country, with the top countries being the United Kingdom, New Zealand, China, India, Italy, Vietnam, and the Philippines.[6] Australia has significantly broadened its social and cultural profile since the days of its "White Australia" policy. These immigrants have greatly enriched Australian society in business, the arts, cooking, science, sports, and many more areas.

Australia opened up immigration laws and now welcomes a more diverse population.

DEMOGRAPHICS

More than two-thirds of the country's current population falls between the ages of 15 and 64 years, with just slightly more men than women (7.5 million compared to 7.3 million). Newborns to 14-year-olds make up the next largest population group at 18.3 percent. Senior citizens, people 65 years and older, account for 14 percent of Australia's population.[7]

In 2012, the estimated life expectancy was 79.48 years for men and 84.45 years for women. At an average of 81.9 years, Australia has a life expectancy that ranks ninth in the world.[8] The birthrate in Australia in 2012 was 12.28 births per 1,000 citizens compared to a death rate of 6.94 deaths per 1,000 citizens, resulting in a population growth rate of 1.126 percent.[9]

AUSTRALIANISMS

Certain British terms are used in Australian English. These include petrol instead of gasoline, the boot instead of the trunk of a car, and telly instead of television. But most noticeable to foreign English-speaking tourists is the vast array of peculiar Australian idioms and expressions that confound Americans and other non-Australian English speakers. If an Australian invites you to "Av-a-go-yer-mug," they are encouraging you to try something or put more effort into it. "Having a blue" means engaging in a fight or argument. "She'll be apples!" is a common Australian phrase assuring the recipient that everything will be all right. The language has also incorporated words of Aboriginal origin, such as kangaroo, wallaby, billabong, boomerang, and dingo.

LANGUAGE

Though Australia does not have an official language, English is the first language of nearly 80 percent of the population.[10] Other languages spoken in Australia include Chinese, Italian, Greek, Arabic, and Vietnamese.

At one time, there were nearly 260 Aboriginal languages. Approximately 145 are still spoken today.[11] An estimated 50,000 Aborigines still speak native Australian languages, but most of the surviving languages have very few speakers, and the vast majority of these native languages have become extinct.[12] However, Aborigines have been working hard to preserve their languages, recording as much as they can from older speakers and teaching Aboriginal youth.

YOU SAY IT!

American English	Australian English
Hello	G'day! (G-die)
Afternoon	Arvo (ah-vo)
Swimsuit	Swimmers
True, genuine	Fair dinkum
Breakfast	Brekkie
Work	Yakka
The Outback or wilderness	Bush
Good for you, well done	Good on ya!
An equal chance	Fair go
Disappear for a while, usually wandering	Go walkabout

Many Aborigines are trying to keep their native languages alive.

Australia does not have different accents throughout the country to the degree that the United States does. However, there are three different forms of pronunciation in Australia: cultivated Australian, broad Australian, and general Australian.

RELIGION

The Australian constitution allows freedom of religion. The majority of Australians are Christians, with the largest denominations being Protestant and Roman Catholic. This mirrors the religious affiliations of the European countries immigrants came from. Large numbers of Italian and Irish immigrants helped boost the ranks of Roman Catholics. In 1977 the Uniting Church was formed when Methodist, Presbyterian, and Congregationalist churches merged to form one larger church body.

Approximately 2 percent of Australian citizens are Buddhist, and another 2 percent adhere to Islam.[13] Melbourne has the largest population of Greeks outside of Greece, and many in that community belong to the Greek Orthodox Church.

Australia also has a growing population of people who either do not claim a specific religion or are not willing to disclose it on the census. In the 2006 census, more than 11 percent of Australians were of an unspecified religion, and a further 18 percent claimed to have no religion.[14]

SPIRITUAL LIFE OF THE ABORIGINES

Similar to many religions, Aboriginal religion includes the belief in supreme beings that formed people and the environment during a period of creation. But instead of worshipping an unseen god, Aboriginal people pray to things that they see in their world. These may take the form of certain landscape features: rocks, plants, or animals. There is no one deity covering all of the tribes across Australia. Instead, each tribe has its own gods, with some overlap of beliefs among tribes. Stories of certain spirits, such as the Rainbow Serpent, are told in many Aboriginal tribes. Its movements across the land are said to have carved out rivers and formed mountain ranges.

ABORIGINAL MEDICINE AND RITUALS

Aborigines believe that evil spirits are the cause of illness and accidents. Healers use chants and songs to cure sickness. Aborigines take part in ceremonies or rituals to invoke ancestral beings to ensure a supply of food and water. They also take part in important initiation ceremonies for boys and girls when they reach adulthood. These can last for weeks and include singing, dancing, storytelling, and the display of body painting and decoration. These gatherings are called corroborees and can include several tribes. Some of these gatherings are private and only involve members of the tribe or family, while others include all within that language group.

The Aborigines interpret dreams as being memories of things that took place during the period of creation. They believe that dreams link them and transport them back to that ancestral time. The term "The Dreamtime" now refers generally to the period of creation.

Many Aboriginal tribes have different beliefs and ceremonies.

CHAPTER 6

CULTURE: VARIED ROOTS

At one time, a significant percentage of Australians could trace their ancestry to prisoners transported to the Australian penal colonies. Australia was unusual in that it was a new nation established by the banished. Adding to the country's peculiar beginnings was the fact that the settlers found themselves surrounded by landscapes and cultures very different from the ones they had left behind. Since that time, people from many different cultures have arrived in Australia. This diversity has led to wide-ranging influences on music, film, theater, dance, literature, and other forms of art.

Australia is home to more than 140 cultural groups.

Flinders Street Station, built in the early twentieth century, is one of Melbourne's architectural landmarks.

THE DIDGERIDOO

The didgeridoo is an Aboriginal musical instrument made from the trunk of a eucalyptus tree. Didgeridoo craftsmen search for trees that have been hollowed out by termites. The tree is then cut down and cleaned, and the bark is removed before the instrument is shaped. Some didgeridoos are painted using traditional Aboriginal designs and techniques. Instruments vary in length from 3 to 10 feet (1 to 3 m). The didgeridoo is played by vibrating the lips against the mouthpiece on one end of the instrument to produce a droning sound. Traditionally, only Aboriginal males play the didgeridoo in ceremonies.

MUSIC

As far back as the nineteenth century, Australia has introduced many talented singers, bands, and instrumentalists to the world stage. In the late nineteenth century, Dame Nellie Melba became an internationally renowned opera singer. In the 1960s, another Australian opera singer, Dame Joan Sutherland, was met with worldwide success, winning a Grammy Award.

In terms of popular music, Olivia Newton-John, Helen Reddy, and the Bee Gees rose to fame in the 1970s. Both hard and soft rock bands, such as Men at Work, INXS, Midnight Oil, and Air Supply, played on international airwaves in the 1980s and 1990s. Heavy metal rock band AC/DC, formed in 1973, shot to international superstardom with their 1980 album *Back in Black.* By 2010,

An aboriginal man plays a didgeridoo.

the album had sold more than 49 million copies worldwide.[1] The group was inducted into the Rock and Roll Hall of Fame in March 2003.

Kylie Minogue, a native of Melbourne, was a teenage soap opera star before becoming a famous pop singer. Singer-songwriter and performer Keith Urban, born in New Zealand but raised in Australia, is a country music star who now lives in the United States and has won a number of music awards. Other major Australian rock acts include Wolfmother, The Temper Trap, and Powderfinger, while Hilltop Hoods and Bliss n Eso are big names in the hip-hop scene. In 2011, breakout Australian indie rock artist Gotye achieved considerable international success.

Aboriginal singers have also gained success in Australia. The group Yothu Yindi came to prominence in the 1980s and 1990s, blending modern rock sounds with traditional instruments such as didgeridoos and native percussion instruments. Geoffrey Gurrumul Yunupingu, formerly of Yothu Yindi, has achieved

ARCHITECTURE

Early architecture in Australia was influenced by the origins of those who came there. The British brought with them Gothic and Tudor styles, while those from other nationalities tried to imitate the architecture of their homelands. Melbourne, a city of heavy European influence, is home to the most European architectural feel in Australia. The Sydney Opera House is a world-renowned sample of modern architecture and innovation.

great success as a solo artist. Blind since birth, Yunupingu sings in his native Yolngu language.

MOVIES

Hollywood features a host of Aussie actors that regularly grace the silver screen. Nicole Kidman, Hugh Jackman, Cate Blanchett, Geoffrey Rush, Eric Bana, Naomi Watts, Hugo Weaving, Toni Collette, Guy Pearce, and the late Heath Ledger, among many others, have all appeared in films both in their native Australia as well as in the United States. Mel Gibson, although born in the United States, later moved to Australia as a teenager. He began his acting career there and was first seen by many in the popular *Mad Max* films shot in Australia. Russell Crowe, a New Zealander by birth, moved to Australia when he was four. He was awarded an Academy Award for best actor for his portrayal of the Roman general Maximus in the 2000 film *Gladiator*.

Australian director and producer Baz Luhrmann is known for his highly stylized films, including *Moulin Rouge!*, *Romeo + Juliet*, *Strictly Ballroom*, and *Australia*. Peter Weir, another famous Australian director, made a name for himself with the films *Picnic at Hanging Rock* and *Gallipoli*. He went on to direct US box office hits *Witness*, *Dead Poets Society*, *The Truman Show*, and *Master and Commander*, all of which were nominated for Academy Awards.

Other important award-nominated Australian films include *Rabbit-Proof Fence, Shine,* and *The Man From Snowy River.* Such family films as *Babe* and *Happy Feet* are the products of Australian filmmakers as well.

Australia's vibrant art scene also includes a strong dedication to the performing arts. The Sydney Opera House is home to the Opera Australia, the Australian Ballet, the Sydney Theatre Company, and the Sydney Symphony Orchestra and hosts more than 1,500 performances every year.[2] The Australian Council for the Arts is a government agency that supports the national opera and ballet, as well as other events throughout the country. Additionally, each state capital has its own symphony orchestra.

LITERATURE

Australia's landscape has been the inspiration for stories, songs, and poems. Europeans were enthralled with early stories of the country's exotic scenery and wildlife. In 1830, *Quintus Servinton* became the first Australian novel to be published. It told the story of the life of a convict. Marcus Clarke's *For the Term of His Natural Life* (1874) also detailed the wretched existence of an Australian prisoner.

Henry Lawson penned short folk stories, songs, and poems in the bush ballad genre. These works dealt with life in the Outback and were popular during the nineteenth century. Andrew Barton "Banjo" Paterson was another famous writer specializing in bush ballads. His "Waltzing Matilda," a song about a person traveling through the Outback, first appeared in a collection of verse in 1917 and went on to become a beloved Australian song. Nevil Shute's novel *A Town Like Alice* (1950) also deals with the struggles of life in the Outback.

Thomas Keneally, a famous Australian author, wrote the novel *Schindler's Ark*, on which the 1993 Steven Spielberg film *Schindler's List* is based. He also wrote the novels *The Chant of Jimmie Blacksmith* and *Confederates*, as well as a nonfiction book on Australian history, *A Commonwealth of Thieves*.

"WALTZING MATILDA"

This popular bush ballad written by Banjo Paterson in 1895 has become known worldwide and is much beloved by Australians. The lyrics for "Waltzing Matilda" are full of distinctive Australian words, as the song tells of a traveling worker (swagman) who makes a cup of tea at his bush camp by a stagnant lake (billabong), captures a sheep (jumbuck) to eat, and then is caught by the sheep's owner (squatter) and three policemen. The title of the song is Australian slang meaning to travel on foot with one's belongings slung over one's back in a "matilda" (bag). The song has its very own museum, the Waltzing Matilda Centre in Winton, Queensland. According to Australia's National Film and Sound Archive, there are more recordings of "Waltzing Matilda" than any other Australian song.

Australia has had one Nobel Prize winner for literature. Patrick White was awarded the prize in 1973. His novels include *The Tree of Life*, *Voss*, and *Riders in the Chariot*, along with numerous plays and short stories. Peter Carey is a well-known Australian novelist whose books

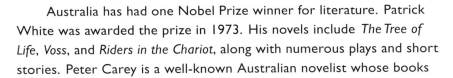

include *True History of the Kelly Gang* and *Oscar and Lucinda*. Many feel he will be the next Australian contender for a Nobel Prize in Literature.

ARTS AND CRAFTS

Australia's art history begins with the Aboriginal people and Torres Strait Islanders. Their paintings on rock walls, tree bark, and wood date as far back as 30,000 years. Their paints were crafted from ocher, a ground-up, reddish, mineral-rich clay that was mixed with water. These early artists sometimes used an "X-ray" style of painting that depicted the subjects' bones and internal organs. Some of these paintings still exist on canyon walls and in caves.

British colonists brought with them a European sense of art. In the nineteenth century, the impressionist style became popular in Australia. By the 1880s, the Heidelberg School of artists, working in the Melbourne suburb of Heidelberg, had emerged. Influenced by French impressionists, these artists' outdoor paintings aimed at capturing light, color, and atmosphere.

Sir Russell Drysdale (1912–1981) became a very famous modern painter, capturing rural Australia with its dramatic, stark landscapes. At the same time, Sir Sidney Nolan (1917–1992) became popular for his surreal paintings of Australian legends, including a 27-painting series

Aborigine art uses ocher to create drawings on rock walls.

Outlaws have a way of becoming legendary, whether it is England's Robin Hood or America's Al Capone. Australia has Ned Kelly. Kelly (1855–1880) was a colonial highwayman known as a bushranger. He was born to an Irish father who was a convict and murderer, and he became a symbol of resistance against the ruling class in Australia. Kelly clashed with the police in 1878 and killed three policemen who were searching for him in the bush. He and the men with him, the Kelly Gang, were declared outlaws. A final confrontation happened in Glenrowan on June 27, 1880. Kelly and his gang were surrounded in a pub. He emerged from the pub wearing homemade metal armor and a helmet, but his legs were unprotected. After being shot in the leg, he was captured and arrested. He was soon tried and hanged for murder. He has become an iconic folk hero in Australian history and is the subject of literature, art, and film.

about Ned Kelly, a famous Australian outlaw from the mid-nineteenth century.

SPORTS

Australians love to play and watch various sporting events. Children start playing at an early age in elementary school. Every town has amateur teams. Australia has more than 120 national sporting organizations and thousands of state and local teams.[3]

As in many countries, soccer is popular. But footy, or Australian rules football, is the most watched sport in the country. Footy is a uniquely Australian sport dating back to the

A player reaches for the ball in a September 2011 Australian rules football match in Melbourne.

mid-nineteenth century and can be roughly described as a combination of soccer and American football.

The British brought cricket, a game that is played with bats and a ball, with them to Australia. Rugby, a game related to American football, was also imported from Britain. Both are very popular in Australia. Australia is one of the top cricketing nations in the world, and its national cricket team has won the World Cup a record four times.

Australia is home to tennis's Australian Open, which is held in Melbourne and is one of the sport's four Grand Slam events. Evonne Goolagong, an Aborigine woman from New South Wales, became a world-famous tennis player, winning 13 Grand Slam titles, including four Australian Opens, from 1971 to 1980.[4] Other Australian tennis stars include Margaret Smith Court, Rod Laver, and Lleyton Hewitt.

Surfing, swimming, boating, yachting, golfing, basketball, cycling, and other outdoor activities are also popular in sunny Australia. Skiing is enjoyed in the higher elevations of Victoria and New South Wales.

Australians have represented their country in the modern Summer Olympics since they began in 1896. In 2000, Sydney was chosen to host the Summer Olympics. The games were held the last two weeks of September. That year, Australian athletes won 16 gold medals, 25 silver medals, and 17 bronze medals.[5]

However, for many years Australia has struggled to bring home gold from the Winter Olympics. The country was first represented at the winter games in 1936. It was not until 2002 that Australia won gold, when Steven Bradbury took first place in the 1,000-meter short track speed skating event and Alisa Camplin did the same in aerial skiing. Torah Bright became a household name when she won gold in half-pipe snowboarding at the 2010 Winter Olympics in Vancouver, Canada.

NATIONAL HOLIDAYS

Public holidays vary slightly from state to state in Australia, but all of Australia celebrates New Year's Day, Australia Day (January 26), Good Friday, Easter Saturday and Easter Monday, Anzac Day (April 25), Christmas Day, and Boxing Day (December 26). Each state has its own Labour Day, but the date varies from state to state.

The Queen's birthday is also celebrated as a national holiday, but the holiday does not occur on the actual birthday of the monarch. Different countries choose different dates on which to honor the Queen. Australia observes the holiday on the second Monday in June each year.

Additionally, states have their own public holidays, such as Victoria's Melbourne Cup Day (the first Tuesday in November). This holiday is held to celebrate the Melbourne Cup, a major horseracing event. Due to its popularity, the race is known as "the event that stops a nation."[6]

AUSSIE CUISINE

Australian cuisine has reaped the benefits of increased immigration. Not long ago, "Australian cuisine" meant little more than meat pies and Vegemite sandwiches. However, the influx of Mediterranean, Asian, and Middle Eastern immigrants has broadened and refined the Australian palate. Italian, Greek, Chinese, Lebanese, Turkish, Balkan, Hungarian, Indian, and Spanish cuisines inspire many everyday Australian meals.

Seafood is plentiful in Australia. Kangaroo and emu meat are specialty meats that are infrequently consumed. More commonly eaten are beef, poultry, and a host of fruits and vegetables. Bananas, pineapple, papayas, mangoes, and the native *quandong*, a wild peach, are staples of the Australian diet.

Vegemite, a black, salty yeast spread that many Australians grow up eating and which some foreigners and Australians find unappetizing, is perhaps the best-known Australian food product. Another local food is lamingtons, a sponge cake cube covered with chocolate and coconut. Barbecue grills, often called barbies, are commonly found in Australian homes, and because of the warm climate, many Australians love to grill their food outdoors.

Vegemite is a well-known Australian spread.

CHAPTER 7

POLITICS: QUEEN AND PARLIAMENT

The Commonwealth of Australia, as the country is officially called, is a constitutional monarchy. This means the country has a monarch as well as a written constitution defining the government's powers and procedures. In 2012, the nation's monarch was Queen Elizabeth II of the United Kingdom. She is formally Australia's queen and head of state, though she has little real power over the nation's affairs.

The monarch appoints a governor-general for Australia. This person's role is largely ceremonial; he or she signs legislation into law and represents the nation on behalf of the monarch but has little actual power. In 2012, this position was held by Quentin Bryce, the first female governor-general in the nation's history.

Queen Elizabeth II and Julia Gillard arrive at a reception at Australian Parliament in 2011.

THE STOLEN GENERATIONS

Beginning in the early twentieth century, it became a standard government practice to take Aboriginal children, particularly those who were of mixed race, from their Aboriginal relatives and place them with white families to be raised apart from the Aboriginal culture. It was felt that integrating them into white society would be for their own good. Some were placed in schools or missions. Oftentimes, these children ended up acting as domestic servants. Most would never see their families again.

The injustices done to "the stolen generations" continued until the 1970s. At that time, the practice was abandoned. But it was not until April 1997, when it released a report entitled *Bringing Them Home*, that the Australian government admitted the wrongs it had done.

In 2008, Prime Minister Kevin Rudd made a formal apology to the Aborigines before the House of Parliament, admitting, "Between 1910 and 1970, between 10 and 30 percent of Indigenous children were forcibly taken from their mothers and fathers. … As a result, up to 50,000 children were forcibly taken from their families."[1] Rudd committed the government to a goal of reducing the gaps in achievement and welfare between Aborigines and other Australians.

Australia is similar to the United States in that a group of states are joined together to form one federation. Each of the six states and two territories has its own government and creates its own laws. However, the federal government handles matters such as defense and foreign relations. Power is divided between the central government and the individual states. Government is divided into three branches: legislative, executive, and judicial.

The country's constitution was agreed to and signed by Queen Victoria on July 9, 1900. It took effect on January 1, 1901. The original document, the Commonwealth of Australia

Former prime minister Kevin Rudd, *right*, apologizes to victims of the Stolen Generations.

Constitution Act 1900, was kept in London at the Public Records Office. In 1990, while the document was on loan to Australia, the Australian government requested permission to keep it. Queen Elizabeth II and the

British parliament agreed, gifting the document to Australia to remain there as part of the nation's history. It is currently on display at the Federation Gallery at the National Archives of Australia in Canberra.

STRUCTURE OF THE GOVERNMENT OF AUSTRALIA

The Executive	Parliament	The Judiciary	Honorary
Prime Minister	Senate	High Court of Australia	Head of State (monarch)
Cabinet	House of Representatives	Federal Court	Governor-General
		Family Court	

BRANCHES OF GOVERNMENT

It is the responsibility of the legislative branch to make laws. This branch of government is made up of the Senate and the House of Representatives. Together, these two bodies comprise the Australian Parliament. The Senate consists of 76 members elected by the people of Australia. Senators representing Australia's states serve six-year

Prime Minister Julia Gillard was first elected to the Australian Parliament in 1998.

THE FLAGS OF AUSTRALIA

The Australian flag features the British flag, consisting of a red and white cross on top of a red and white diagonal cross, in the upper left corner atop a background of dark blue. Below this is a white, seven-pointed star that symbolizes the six states plus the Northern Territory. On the right side of the flag is the constellation Crux, or the Southern Cross as it is often called, which is the most distinguishable constellation in the Southern Hemisphere.

Australia's Aborigines have their own official flag. It features a yellow sun atop black and red horizontal panels. The black signifies the Aboriginal people, and the red signifies the land.

terms, while senators from Australia's territories serve three-year terms. Each state elects 12 senators and the two territories each elect two. The House of Representatives is comprised of 150 members who are elected by the populace to three-year terms.

Australia's executive branch of government is comprised of a prime minister and a cabinet. The prime minister is the head of Australia's government; the role exists by convention and is not mentioned in the Australian Constitution. The political party with the most seats in the House of Representatives appoints the prime minister, who then selects members of the cabinet, which is comprised of members of Parliament. Each cabinet member minister is in charge

The Australian flag

of a separate area of policy, such as defense or immigration. Julia Eileen Gillard became Australia's prime minister in June 2010 as a member of the Labor Party. She was the first woman to serve in this capacity in Australian history.

General elections take place every three years. Citizens may vote at age 18. Voting is mandatory, and those who do not vote are subject to a small fine.

The judicial branch of Australia's government is its court system. The nation's highest court is the High Court of Australia. The High Court has a chief justice and six other justices; all are appointed by the prime minister and cabinet. Appointed justices are allowed to serve until they are 70 years old. Court cases are heard first in the courts of their respective state or territory. Appealed cases can then proceed all the way up to the High Court, the decisions of which are final. Australia's Federal Court deals with court cases involving banking, trade, and industry, while the Family Court decides cases regarding matters such as divorce and child custody.

STATE AND LOCAL GOVERNMENT

Each of Australia's states has a governor, a premier, and a parliament. The premier is head of government for that state while the governor is the representative for the British monarch. By contrast, territories only have an administrator and parliament. These state and territorial governments are responsible for matters such as public education, roads, police, and public health, which are funded in part by the federal government.

The local governments of shires, cities, and towns oversee public issues such as collecting fees, maintaining roads, and collecting garbage. Local government handles libraries, fire prevention, parks and recreation, and other local matters.

MAJOR POLITICAL PARTIES

Although Australia has three major political parties, two of these often form a coalition during national elections.

The Australian Labor Party (ALP), a center-left group that supports social democracy, is a strong ally of trade unions. The prime minister in 2012, Julia Eileen Gillard, belonged to the ALP. The ALP has been a major party for more than a decade. The Liberal Party, led by Tony Abbott, has a philosophy of conservative social policies and liberal economic policies. This party is often joined by the National Party, which represents rural interests, specifically agriculture. Since 1910, every

elected prime minister has been a member of either the Labor Party, the Liberal Party, or one of the former parties that are now part of the Liberal Party.

Another smaller party that has gained a significant following is the Australian Greens, a left-wing party focused on environmental concerns. Christine Milne is the current leader of the Australian Greens.

MILITARY

The Australian Defence Force (ADF), Australia's military, consists of the Royal Australian Navy (RAN), the Australian Army, the Royal Australian Air Force (RAAF), and Special Operations Command.

While there is no mandatory military service in Australia, young men and women can volunteer at the age of 17 with parental consent. Women are allowed to serve in the military but only in noncombat support roles.

In 2012, approximately 3,300 ADF personnel were serving overseas on 14 different operations in locations such as Afghanistan, East Timor, Egypt, and the Middle East.[3]

Australian troops contributed to the efforts of the United States and other allies in Afghanistan.

CHAPTER 8

ECONOMICS: RICH IN RESOURCES

In 2008, a global recession hit countries worldwide. Many nations experienced economic struggles as increasing unemployment rates, falling home values, and rising petroleum and food prices took their toll. By December 2010, the unemployment rate in the United States hit 9.8 percent.[1] The United Kingdom reached a rate of 7.9 percent the following month.[2]

But while countries around the world watched unemployment lines grow, Australia was one of very few nations that kept its unemployment rates relatively low. Over the years, Australia has established strong export ties with China. Continued Chinese demand for Australian commodities helped the country weather the global financial crisis and rebound after only a brief period of negative growth. In 2012, Australia's economy continued to be strong.

The central business district of Melbourne. Australia's economy has proven more resilient than those of many of its global neighbors.

THE AUSTRALIAN DOLLAR

Australia's currency is the Australian Dollar, adopted in 1966. Prior to that year, Australia used the Australian Pound, which had been introduced in 1910. Based on the British Pound, the Australian pound (A£) consisted of 20 shillings, with each shilling consisting of 12 pence. In 1966, Australia introduced the Australian dollar, which was divided into 100 cents, making transactions simpler than under the pound system.

In 1988, the Reserve Bank of Australia introduced a revolutionary type of banknote made of polypropylene polymer, a type of plastic. The change made currency more durable and more difficult to counterfeit. Today, all denominations of Australian banknotes (5, 10, 20, 50, and 100) are made of polymer. The banknotes feature portraits of notable people from Australian history. Different denominations have slightly different sizes, making it easier for visually impaired people to distinguish them.

The Australian Dollar (AUD) is the official currency of Australia, Christmas Island, the Cocos (Keeling) Islands, and Norfolk Island. Australia's economic stability in difficult times has made the Australian Dollar a popular currency with investors.

THE LABOR FORCE AND UNEMPLOYMENT

In 2012, Australia had fewer than 11.5 million people in the country's labor force, constituting a participation rate of just over 65 percent.[3] The participation rate is the number of people of

Australian currency

working age who are either working or looking for work, divided by the total number of people of working age. The unemployment rate was 5.2 percent.[4] The per capita gross domestic product, the nation's total production divided by its population, was estimated at $40,800 in 2011, which ranks nineteenth in the world.[5]

A country's poverty rates are typically calculated by setting a poverty line at a particular income level and then determining how many people fall below that line. Australia, however, does not have an established poverty line. But that does not mean there are no Australians who live in poverty. According to the Organisation for Economic Cooperation and Development, 20 percent of Australian households have earnings totaling less than 60 percent of the average household income.[6]

MINING AND MANUFACTURING EXPORTS

Australia is rich in natural resources. In the 1960s, mining operations began extracting resources from vast iron ore ranges in the Hamersley Range, extensive bauxite reserves in the Darling Ranges, and high-grade coal resources at Mount Arthur, as well as nickel, copper, uranium, oil, and natural gas. Over the course of the following decades, mining grew to become a large part of the Australian economy. Currently, minerals account for approximately one-third of the country's exports.[7] Australia is among the top exporters of coal, iron ore, lead, and diamonds. Other exports include meat, wool, aluminum, wheat, machinery, and transport equipment. Australia's export partners include China, Japan, South Korea, India, and the United States. Australia imports machinery,

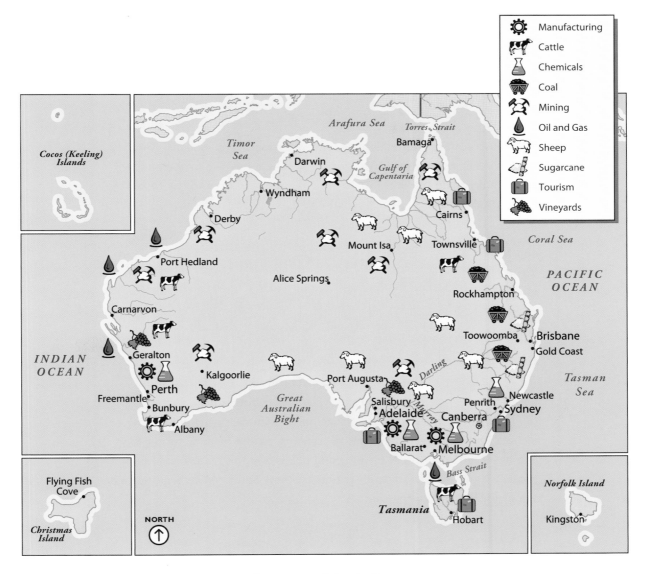

Legend

- ⚙ Manufacturing
- 🐄 Cattle
- ⚗ Chemicals
- ⬛ Coal
- ⛏ Mining
- 🛢 Oil and Gas
- 🐑 Sheep
- Sugarcane
- 🧳 Tourism
- 🍇 Vineyards

Cocos (Keeling) Islands

Arafura Sea

Timor Sea

Bamaga

Darwin

Gulf of Capentaria

Wyndham

Derby

Cairns

Port Hedland

Mount Isa

Townsville

Coral Sea

PACIFIC OCEAN

Carnarvon

Alice Springs

Rockhampton

INDIAN OCEAN

Geralton

Kalgoorlie

Toowoomba

Brisbane

Perth

Port Augusta

Darling

Newcastle

Tasman Sea

Freemantle

Bunbury

Great Australian Bight

Salisbury

Murray

Penrith

Sydney

Albany

Adelaide

Canberra

Ballarat

Melbourne

Gold Coast

Bass Strait

Flying Fish Cove

Norfolk Island

Christmas Island

NORTH
↑

Tasmania

Hobart

Kingston

Resources of Australia

telecommunication equipment, crude oil, petroleum products, and computers and office machines from countries such as China, Japan, Thailand, Singapore, Germany, and Malaysia.

Australia has tremendous reserves of natural gas, much of which is sold to Asian countries. In Western Australia, a massive project known as Gorgon Liquid Natural Gas promises to further expand the resources sector in Australia.

The finest opals in the world come from sites in South Australia and New South Wales. Deposits of rare black opals are found in Lightning Ridge in New South Wales, and sapphires and topaz are mined in Queensland and New South Wales. Australia also mines gold and is among the world's largest producers. Most of the country's output comes from Western Australian mines. Silver is extracted from the districts of Broken Hill and Mount Isa.

Japanese and American car manufacturers have assembly and full-production plants in Australia, which contribute a major source of employment in large cities. Other major manufacturing industries include iron and steel, chemicals, oil refining, textile manufacturing, food and beverage production, printing and publishing, machinery and metal products, and wood and paper products. New South Wales and Victoria are major manufacturing centers.

CROPS AND LIVESTOCK

Generally, Australia has very poor soil conditions for growing crops. Average rainfall, especially in the country's interior, is far too low. Barley, wheat, oats, cotton, rice, tobacco, tropical fruits, corn sorghum, oilseed, and other crops are planted on usable areas. Sugarcane thrives in the northern tropical region of Australia and is the country's second-largest export. These crops contribute approximately 4 percent of Australia's GDP.[8] Additionally, vineyards and winemaking have experienced spectacular growth in the recent past. Grapes are grown in every state, but they thrive particularly well in the southern areas of the country.

Since the early nineteenth century, sheep have been an important

AUSTRALIA'S GROWING WINE INDUSTRY

Although Australia has no native grape varieties suitable for winemaking, the First Fleet brought cuttings from grapevines to plant in Australia. Dating back to the 1790s, settlers successfully grew grapes, produced wine, and sent it back to Great Britain. Today, more than 200 years later, Australia is one of the world's leading wine producers. Since it is such a large country with varied soil types and climates, a wide variety of grapes thrive in Australia, making it possible to produce all major types of wines.

Australian wine is exported and sold in more than 100 countries worldwide. The United Kingdom currently imports more wine from Australia than from France. On average, Australia exports approximately 200 million gallons (750 million L) of wine per year.[9]

Australian industry. During Great Britain's industrial revolution, half of the wool it used to produce cloth was imported from Australia. Currently, wool and beef are the country's major farm products. Australia is still the world's leader in the production and export of wool. Farmers raise sheep and cattle on large ranches called stations, the majority of which are found in New South Wales, Queensland, and Western Australia. Sheep stations can have as many as 100,000 sheep at one location. The majority of Australia's raw wool exports, more than 80 percent, go to China.[10]

In the 2009 season, 73 million sheep were shorn in Australia.

THE SERVICE AND TOURISM INDUSTRY

The largest percentage of employed Australians—more than 75 percent—works in the services industries, which include professions such as finance, transport, trade, education, and insurance. Australia's service industry accounts for more than 70 percent of the GDP.[11]

Due to its isolated location, Australia receives fewer visitors than many other countries. However, tourism accounts for 5 percent of the GDP and provides employment to approximately 5 percent of the work force.[12] Nearly 5 million tourists visit Australia yearly from overseas.

Sugarcane is an important crop in Australia.

LIFE UNDERGROUND IN COOBER PEDY

Halfway between Adelaide and Alice Springs in northern South Australia is the small town of Coober Pedy. Often called the opal capital of the world, this small, desert mining town is home to approximately 2,000 residents. Because temperatures become extremely hot in the summer months, people dig caves into the hillsides called dugouts. These dwellings remain at a constant moderate temperature despite how hot the summer months get, meaning there is no need to cool these dugout homes. In addition to residential homes, Coober Pedy also has underground churches, art galleries, and a four-star luxury hotel.

Most come from New Zealand, Japan, the United Kingdom, the United States, and Singapore.[13]

RAIL, ROAD, AND AIR TRAVEL

Transportation in Australia has taken an interesting journey. In the 1860s, Europeans brought camels to Australia to help with traversing and exploring the vast Australian deserts. Expert camel drivers from Afghanistan were brought in to handle the animals. Named in their honor, the Afghan Railway runs the path of the old camel routes from Adelaide to Alice Springs and now continues on to Darwin on the north shore, connecting the continent by rail from north to south. The journey takes two days and covers 1,851 miles (2,979 km).[14]

Although it can be difficult for people to visit Australia, it is a popular place for tourism.

The Indian Pacific Railway connects the continent from east to west, running from Perth in the west to Sydney in the east. This route, which takes three days to travel, is the country's longest train route. Australia also has freight train routes that carry farm, mining, and production products into coastal cities where they can be loaded onto ships for export. Melbourne and Sydney have railways, trams, and commuter passenger trains.

THE FLYING DOCTOR

Medical service in the Outback was difficult until 1928, when an experiment called Aerial Medical Service was launched. Based out of Cloncurry in Queensland, this service was formed by Reverend John Flynn of the Presbyterian Church of Australia. Flynn was a missionary who worked to establish hospitals in bush communities. Prior to the AMS, injured people far from populated communities would have to endure long, difficult journeys over land to reach medical attention. Today, "The Flying Doctor" offers emergency and primary health care services to Australians living in remote regions.

National highways connect large cities in Australia, and modern expressways and throughways are becoming more commonplace in larger capital cities. Though some paved roads exist in the country's interior, dirt roads are standard throughout most of the Outback.

Flying is a safe and economical travel option in Australia, given the great distances across inhospitable land regions people must travel to get from one region to the other. Qantas Airlines (which takes its name from a shortened form of Queensland and Northern Territory Aerial Services) is the country's national airline. The busiest international airport is located in Sydney, with others in Melbourne, Darwin, Hobart, Cairns, and Canberra. Hundreds of other smaller airports connect Australia, supporting flights from city to city, as well as into and out of the Outback.

CHAPTER 9
AUSTRALIA TODAY

Daily life in Australia is very similar to life in the United States. Most households consist of parents and their children, but do not include older generations or extended families. Most couples have one or two children, and both parents typically work outside the home.

In recent years, there has been an increase in the number of children born to unmarried parents. In 1990, 22 percent of children were born to unmarried parents, but that rate rose to 34 percent in 2010.[1] As many as 77 percent of couples live together before they get married.[2]

Australia boasts a literacy rate of 99 percent.

EDUCATION IN AUSTRALIA

Australian children are very well educated. Australians typically begin school at age four. They enter into kindergarten and move on

The average family in Australia typically consists of parents and one or two children.

to primary school, which includes grades 1 through 7 (roughly ages five through 12). Middle school includes grades 7 through 9 (ages 12 to 15). High school, known as college in Tasmania and the Australian Capital Territory, covers grades 10 through 12.

Students study a broad range of subjects, including math, science, English, social sciences, and foreign languages. Many Australian children wear uniforms to school. Public schools are government funded and are run according to the laws of the state or territory. Approximately two-thirds of students attend public schools.[3] Australia also has private schools, many of which are affiliated with the Roman Catholic Church. There are also Jewish, Islamic, Protestant, and other religious schools.

TALL POPPY SYNDROME

Australians do not look too fondly on those who try to brag about their achievements. In fact, it is discouraged and called the "Tall Poppy Syndrome." As one author noted in a book on Australian culture, "However . . . should [someone achieve] success, fame, and money, he immediately transforms into a Tall Poppy, a most undesirable thing, begging to be cut down to size. The typical Australian tries not to shine too obviously and does not much like those who do. As a result, it's difficult if not impossible to set yourself individual excellence as a goal in Australia."[4]

Australians spend an average of 21 years in school, the most of people in any nation.

Schoolchildren must attend school until age 15, with the exception of Tasmania, which requires students to attend until the age of 16. While the majority of children go through grade 12, those who exit school earlier have the option of entering into apprenticeships or beginning manual labor jobs.

The school year begins in early February and runs through mid-December for primary and secondary schools. Students have their summer break over Christmas. Schools have four terms, separated by two-week breaks.

At the end of grade 12, students take tests that determine their qualifications to

SCHOOL OF THE AIR

Children living in remote regions of Australia are unable to attend regular schools. Therefore, in 1951, the Royal Flying Doctor Service in Adelaide started a program conducting lessons via shortwave radio. Children received materials and returned completed assignments via the Royal Flying Doctor Service. The School of the Air is still active today, although more students utilize the Internet to participate in their lessons. Students spend approximately one hour per day over the radio or online in contact with their teachers through group or individual lessons. Children then spend the remainder of the school day working on homework. Parents and older siblings often help with schoolwork.

Australian schoolchildren greet Queen Elizabeth II in 2011.

go on to one of Australia's 40 universities and technical schools. A student's performance in high school is taken into account when this determination is made. High school graduates typically do not have elaborate graduation ceremonies. They simply finish their tests and say good-bye to their teachers and fellow classmates. Many graduates spend time traveling to countries in the Northern Hemisphere before starting university.

FREE TIME

Australian children enjoy many of the same activities that American children do. They attend movies, go to music concerts, play sports, and often spend ample time at the beach. Some teens hold part-time jobs while going to school. Australians are allowed to get a driver's license at age 17 or 18, depending on the state. Learner's permits can be obtained at age 16 in most states. Australians are allowed to drink alcohol at the age of 18.

> Australia has strict laws against violent video games. Many games are censored or banned.

Playing video games, watching television, and spending time on the Internet have also risen in popularity in the recent past. However, possibly as a result of these sedentary activities, more than one quarter of Australian children are now overweight or obese.[5]

Sports are extremely important to most Australians. Children play on school teams that are divided by age groups. During the summer, many boys play cricket, while during the winter they choose between rugby and Australian rules footy. Netball, a sport similar to basketball, is popular among school-age girls.

CURRENT AND FUTURE CHALLENGES

Although Australia has fared relatively well in the recent global economic crisis, the country still faces challenges. Global instability continues and the long-term implications are as yet unclear. As former prime minister Kevin Rudd pointed out in 2011, "The sheer size, complexity, and interconnectedness of private financial markets now challenge the ability of any individual national government to monitor and properly regulate them."[6]

Although the White Australia policy has been gone for more than three decades, immigration continues to be a debated issue in Australia. Other difficulties include racial discrimination and poor overall health of disadvantaged groups such as Aborigines. Environmental issues, including global climate change, pollution, and harm to the Great Barrier Reef remain high on the list of concerns in Australia.

> Some activists now oppose immigration on environmental grounds, since more people means more pollution.

However, even in the face of these challenges, it seems likely that the Australian people will win out against them. Australia's history has

demonstrated it is a nation of people dedicated to finding solutions and overcoming unfavorable odds.

Damage to the environment was one of the key challenges facing Australia in 2012.

TIMELINE

50,000 BCE	Australian Aborigines come to the Australian continent via land bridges and ocean crossings.
1606	Dutch navigator Willem Janszoon lands on Australian soil.
1616	Dutchman Dirck Hartog explores Shark Bay in Western Australia.
1642	Abel Tasman is the first European to discover the island south of Mainland Australia, later named Tasmania.
1770	Captain James Cook from Britain lands the *HMS Endeavor* in Australia on April 20, claiming the eastern coast for Britain.
1787	The First Fleet leaves England on May 13.
1788	The First Fleet arrives at Botany Bay January 19–20.
1788	The colony of Sydney is officially established on January 26, a date that is celebrated as Australia Day.
1801–1803	British navigator Matthew Flinders sails around the continent of Australia, discovering that the country is an independent landmass.
1851	Gold is discovered in Ballarat and Bendigo in Victoria, kicking off the Australian gold rush.
1859	Australia's colonies are granted self-government from Britain.
1901	On January 1 the Commonwealth of Australia becomes a nation with a new federal government.

1902	Most women (though not Aboriginal women) gain the right to vote.
1908	Canberra is chosen as Australia's capital.
1914–1918	Australia joins the war effort during World War I, volunteering to aid Great Britain.
1939–1945	Australia fights Germany, Italy, and Japan in World War II.
1945	Australia joins the UN as a founding member.
1940s	Australia welcomes large numbers of European immigrants.
1956	Melbourne is host to the Olympic Games.
1959	Construction begins on the Sydney Opera House.
1973	The White Australia policy is abandoned.
1997	The Australian government issues an official apology to the Aboriginal children of the Stolen Generations.
2000	Sydney hosts the 2000 Summer Olympic Games.
2010	Julia Eileen Gillard becomes Australia's first female prime minister.

FACTS AT YOUR FINGERTIPS

GEOGRAPHY

Official name: Commonwealth of Australia

Area: 2,988,901 square miles (7,741,220 sq km)

Climate: Arid desert in the middle two-thirds of the country, tropical in the north, temperate climate in the southern portion of the country

Highest elevation: Mount Kosciusko, 7,310 feet (2,229 m) above sea level

Lowest elevation: Lake Eyre, 53 feet (16 m) below sea level

Significant geographic features: Great Barrier Reef, the Outback

PEOPLE

Population (July 2012 est.): 22,015,576

Most populous city: Sydney

Ethnic groups: White, 92 percent; Asian, 7 percent; Aboriginal and other, 1 percent

Percentage of residents living in urban areas: 90 percent

Life expectancy: 81.9 years at birth (world rank: 9)

Language(s): Australian English

Religion(s): Protestantism, 27.4 percent; Roman Catholicism, 25.8 percent; Eastern Orthodox, 2.7 percent; other forms of Christianity, 7.9 percent; Buddhism, 2.1 percent; Islam, 1.7 percent; unspecified, 11.3 percent; none, 18 percent

GOVERNMENT AND ECONOMY

Government: federal parliamentary democracy

Capital: Canberra

Date of adoption of current constitution: July 9, 1900

Head of state: queen or king

Head of government: prime minister

Legislature: Senate and House of Representatives

Currency: Australian dollar

Industries and natural resources: extensive reserves of coal, iron ore, copper, gold, natural gas, uranium, and renewable energy sources. Chief industries include mining, industrial and transportation equipment, food processing, chemicals, and steel.

NATIONAL SYMBOLS

Holidays: A national holiday on May 3 celebrates the signing of the current constitution.

Flag: The flag of Great Britain in the upper left corner atop a dark blue background. Below the British flag lies a white seven-pointed star, and to the right of that is the constellation *Crux*, or the Southern Cross.

National anthem: "Advance Australia Fair"

National animal: None, but the kangaroo and emu appear on Australia's coat of arms

KEY PEOPLE

Queen Elizabeth II (1926–), head of state of Australia

Julia Eileen Gillard (1961–), prime minster of Australia and first woman to hold the job

STATES AND TERRITORIES OF AUSTRALIA

State; Capital

New South Wales; Sydney

Queensland; Brisbane

South Australia; Adelaide

Tasmania; Hobart

Victoria; Melbourne

Western Australia; Perth

Territory; Capital or largest settlement

Australian Capital Territory; Canberra

Jervis Bay Territory; Jervis Bay Village

Northern Territory; Darwin

Island territory; Capital or largest settlement

Ashmore and Cartier Islands; (uninhabited)

Australian Antarctic Territory; Davis Station

Christmas Island; Flying Fish Cove

Cocos (Keeling) Islands; West Island

Coral Sea Islands; uninhabited

Norfolk Island; Kingston

Territory of Heard Island and McDonald Islands; uninhabited

GLOSSARY

aboriginal
Relating to the native people of Australia.

acacia
Shrubs and trees belonging to the legume family that grow in warm areas and have white or yellow flower clusters.

arid
A region that is excessively dry with insufficient rainfall to support growing crops.

coalition
A group of political parties that join together to govern.

dugong
A water-dwelling mammal, similar to a manatee, that inhabits the warm coastal waters of southern Asia, Australia, and northeastern Africa.

emancipist
A convict who has either fully served his or her term and is set free, or has been granted a pardon or early release.

eucalyptus
Plants and trees of the genus *Eucalyptus* that grow natively in Australia and are used for their gums, oils, resins, and wood.

gestation period
The development stage for mammal offspring, beginning with fertilization and ending with the time of birth.

gross domestic product (GDP)

The total production in a country divided by its population. Used to gauge the wealth of a nation.

indigenous

Something that grows, occurs, or is produced in a given environment or region.

mangroves

Trees and shrubs that grow along coasts in the ocean's saltwater.

monsoon

A rainy season in Northern Australia typically lasting from September to February.

quay

A structure built adjacent to the bank of a waterway that is used as a landing.

reef

A chain of rocks or coral occurring near the surface of the water.

wharf

A structure built alongside a waterway that enables boats and ships to move alongside to be loaded and unloaded.

ADDITIONAL RESOURCES

SELECTED BIBLIOGRAPHY

Berra, Tim M. *A Natural History of Australia*. San Diego, CA: Academic Press, 1998. Print.

Keneally, Thomas. *A Commonwealth of Thieves*. New York: Doubleday, 2006. Print.

Sharp, Ilsa. *CultureShock! Australia: A Survival Guide to Customs and Etiquette*. Tarrytown, NY: Marshall Cavendish Corporation: 2009. Print.

FURTHER READINGS

Darlington, Robert. *Australia*. New York: Raintree Steck-Vaughn Publishers, 2001.

Macintyre, Stuart. *A Concise History of Australia*. New York: Cambridge UP, 2009. Print.

WEB LINKS

To learn more about Australia, visit ABDO Publishing Company online at **www.abdopublishing.com**. Web sites about Australia are featured on our Book Links page. These links are routinely monitored and updated to provide the most current information available.

PLACES TO VISIT

If you are ever in Australia, consider checking out these important and interesting sites!

Great Barrier Reef

This UNESCO World Heritage Site is often called the largest structure built by living organisms. It consists of a series of reefs that run along the northeast coast of Australia offshore in the waters of the Coral Sea. Visitors can explore the Great Barrier Reef from Cairns in Queensland.

Sydney Opera House

This world-famous performance venue is home to the Opera Australia, The Australian Ballet, Sydney Theatre Company, and the Sydney Symphony Orchestra, and hosts more than 1,500 performances every year.

Twelve Apostles

Off the shore of the Port Campbell National Park in Victoria, the limestone pillars of the Twelve Apostles rise out of the Southern Ocean. Sightseers can view this iconic Australian landmark from the Great Ocean Road that winds along the southeast coast of Victoria.

Uluru (Ayers Rock)

Uluru, formerly known as Ayers Rock, is a 1,142-foot (348 m) tall sandstone rock formation that rises out of the desolate desert of central Australia. It is found within Uluru-Kata Tjuta National Park.

SOURCE NOTES

CHAPTER 1. A VISIT TO AUSTRALIA

1. Rita Braver. "Sydney Opera House: Masterpiece of Design." *Sunday Morning.* CBS News, 22 May 2011. Web. 16 Aug. 2012.

CHAPTER 2. GEOGRAPHY: THE LAND DOWN UNDER

1. Richard Macey. "Map from Above Shows Australia Is a Very Flat Place." *Sydney Morning Herald.* Sydney Morning Herald, 22 January 2005. Web. 16 Aug. 2012.

2. Tim Berra. *A Natural History of Australia.* San Diego: Academic Press, 1998. Print. 4.

3. *Tasmania: Gateway to Antarctica.* Tasmania Department of Economic Development, Tourism and the Arts, n.d. Web. 16 Aug. 2012.

4. "The World Factbook: Australia." *Central Intelligence Agency.* Central Intelligence Agency, 10 July 2012. Web. 16 Aug. 2012.

5. Tim Berra. *A Natural History of Australia.* San Diego: Academic Press, 1998. Print. 4.

6. "Australia." *Weatherbase.* Canty and Associates, 2012. Web. 16 Aug. 2012.

7. "Australia." *Encyclopædia Britannica.* Encyclopædia Britannica, 2012. Web. 16 Aug. 2012.

8. Ibid.

9. "Mount Kosciuszko." *Encyclopædia Britannica.* Encyclopædia Britannica, 2012. Web. 16 Aug. 2012.

10. "Murray River." *Encyclopædia Britannica.* Encyclopædia Britannica, 2012. Web. 16 Aug. 2012.

CHAPTER 3. ANIMALS AND NATURE: A UNIQUE ASSORTMENT

1. "Marsupial." *Encyclopædia Britannica.* Encyclopædia Britannica, 2012. Web. 16 Aug. 2012.

2. "Inland Taipan." *Nature: Wildlife.* BBC, 2012. Web. 16 Aug. 2012.

3. "Snake Bite." *Australian Venom Research Unit.* University of Melbourne, 23 Apr. 2012. Web. 16 Aug. 2012.

4. "Indian Snakebite Deaths 23 Times Higher than Thought." *New Scientist.* New Scientist, 8 Dec. 2011. Web. 16 Aug. 2012.

5. "Python Hungers: Cane Toad Madness." *Nat Geo Wild.* National Geographic, 1 May 2012. Web. 16 Aug. 2012.

6. "Great Barrier Reef." *Australia.* World Wildlife Fund, n.d. Web. 16 Aug. 2012.

7. "How Much Is Nature Worth?" *Bloomberg Businessweek.* Bloomberg News, 28 Dec. 2004. Web. 16 Aug. 2012.

8. "Summary Statistics: Summaries by Country, Table 5, Threatened Species in Each Country." *IUCN Red List of Threatened Species*. International Union for Conservation of Nature and Natural Resources, 2011. Web. 16 Aug. 2012.

9. "National Parks." *About Australia*. Australian Government, 11 Mar. 2011. Web. 16 Aug. 2012.

CHAPTER 4. HISTORY: HUMBLE BEGINNINGS

1. "Population Composition: Indigenous Languages." *Bureau of Statistics*. Australian Government, 24 June 1999. Web. 16 Aug. 2012.

2. Thomas Keneally. *A Commonwealth of Thieves*. New York: Anchor Books, 2006. Print. 6.

3. Ibid. 43.

4. "Convict Transportation Registers Database." *State Library of Queensland*. Queensland Government, 13 Apr. 2012. Web. 16 Aug. 2012.

5. "The Australian Gold Rush." *About Australia*. Australian Government, 5 Oct. 2007. Web. 16 Aug. 2012.

6. "First World War." *War History*. Australian War Memorial, n.d. Web. 16 Aug. 2012.

7. Ibid.

8. "Deaths as a Result of Service with Australian Units." *Encyclopedia*. Australian War Memorial, n.d. Web. 16 Aug. 2012.

CHAPTER 5. PEOPLE: A VIBRANT POPULACE

1. "The World Factbook: Australia." *Central Intelligence Agency*. Central Intelligence Agency, 10 July 2012. Web. 16 Aug. 2012.

2. "The World Factbook: The United States." *Central Intelligence Agency*. Central Intelligence Agency, 1 Aug. 2012. Web. 16 Aug. 2012.

3. "The World Factbook: Australia." *Central Intelligence Agency*. Central Intelligence Agency, 10 July 2012. Web. 16 Aug. 2012.

4. "Australia." *Encyclopædia Britannica*. Encyclopædia Britannica, 2012. Web. 16 Aug. 2012.

5. "About." *Department of Health and Ageing*. Australian Government, 4 Feb. 2011. Web. 16 Aug. 2012.

6. "Australian-Born and Overseas-Born." *Bureau of Statistics*. Australian Government, 16 June 2011. Web. 16 Aug. 2012.

7. Ibid.

8. "The World Factbook: Australia." *Central Intelligence Agency*. Central Intelligence Agency, 10 July 2012. Web. 16 Aug. 2012.

9. Ibid.

SOURCE NOTES CONTINUED

10. Ibid.

11. "National Indigenous Languages Policy." *Department of Regional Australia, Local Government, Arts and Sport.* Australian Government, n.d. Web. 16 Aug. 2012.

12. "Australian Aboriginal Languages." *Encyclopædia Britannica.* Encyclopædia Britannica, 2012. Web. 16 Aug. 2012.

13. "The World Factbook: Australia." *Central Intelligence Agency.* Central Intelligence Agency, 10 July 2012. Web. 16 Aug. 2012.

14. Ibid.

CHAPTER 6. CULTURE: VARIED ROOTS

1. James Sullivan. "'None More Black': 30 Years of AC/DC's 'Back in Black.'" *Spinner.* AOL, 22 July 2010. Web. 16 Aug. 2012.

2. "Highlights 2010/2011." *Sydney Opera House.* Sydney Opera House, 2011. Web. 16 Aug. 2012.

3. "People, Culture, and Lifestyle." *Department of Foreign Affairs and Trade.* Australian Government, Feb. 2012. Web. 16 Aug. 2012.

4. "Evonne (Goolagong) Cawley." *Player Profiles.* Tennis Australia, 2012. Web. 16 Aug. 2012.

5. "All the Medalists Since 1896." *Olympic.org.* Olympic.org, 2012. Web. 16 Aug. 2012.

6. "Public Holidays." *Victoria Online.* State Government of Victoria, 16 Aug. 2012. Web. 16 Aug. 2012.

CHAPTER 7. POLITICS: QUEEN AND PARLIAMENT

1. Ilsa Sharp. *CultureShock! Australia: A Survival Guide to Customs and Etiquette.* Tarrytown, NY: Marshall Cavendish, 2009. Print. 113.

2. "Australia and the United Nations." *Department of Foreign Affairs and Trade.* Australian Government, 5 May 2012. Web. 16 Aug. 2012.

3. "Global Operations." *Department of Defence.* Australian Government, 2 May 2012. Web. 16 Aug. 2012.

CHAPTER 8. ECONOMICS: RICH IN RESOURCES

1. Scott Neuman. "U.S. Unemployment Rate Jumps To 9.8 Percent." *NPR.* NPR, 3 Dec. 2010. Web. 16 Aug. 2012

2. "UK Unemployment Total Rises Further." *BBC News Business.* BBC, 19 Jan. 2011. Web. 16 Aug. 2012.

3. "6202.0 – Labour Force, Australia, Apr. 2012." *Bureau of Statistics.* Australian Government, 10 May 2012. Web. 16 Aug. 2012.

4. Ibid.

5. "The World Factbook: Australia." *Central Intelligence Agency*. Central Intelligence Agency, 10 July 2012. Web. 16 Aug. 2012.

6. "Homelessness and Poverty." *Homelessness Australia*. Homelessness Australia, n.d. Web. 16 Aug. 2012.

7. "Australia." *Encyclopædia Britannica*. Encyclopædia Britannica, 2012. Web. 16 Aug. 2012.

8. "The World Factbook: Australia." *Central Intelligence Agency*. Central Intelligence Agency, 10 July 2012. Web. 16 Aug. 2012.

9. "1329.0 –Australian Wine and Grape Industry." *Bureau of Statistics*. Australian Government, 27 Feb. 2012. Web. 16 Aug. 2012.

10. Asa Wahlquist. "Wool Exporters See Market Unravel." *Australian Business*. Australian Business, 25 May 2009. Web. 16 Aug. 2012.

11. "The World Factbook: Australia." *Central Intelligence Agency*. Central Intelligence Agency, 10 July 2012. Web. 16 Aug. 2012.

12. "Key Facts – Tourism." *Department of Resources, Energy and Tourism*. Australian Government, March 2010. Web. 16 Aug. 2012.

13. Ibid.

14. "The Ghan." *Rail Australia*. Rail Australia, 2009. Web. 16 Aug. 2012.

CHAPTER 9. AUSTRALIA TODAY

1. Sue Dunlevy. "One-Third of Infants Born to Unmarried Parents." *Australian*. Australian, 23 Mar. 2012. Web. 16 Aug. 2012.

2. "3306.0.55.001 – Marriages, Australia, 2007." *Bureau of Statistics*. Australian Government, 30 Sept. 2008. Web. 17 Aug. 2012.

3. "4221.0 – Schools, Australia, 2010." *Bureau of Statistics*. Australian Government, 17 Mar. 2011. Web. 17 Aug. 2012.

4. Ilsa Sharp. *CultureShock! Australia: A Survival Guide to Customs and Etiquette*. Tarrytown, NY: Marshall Cavendish: 2009. Print. 269.

5. "4125.0 – Gender Indicators, Australia, 2012." *Bureau of Statistics*. Australian Government, 2 July 2011. Web. 17 Aug. 2012.

6. Kevin Rudd. "The 10 Big Global Challenges Facing Australia." *Sydney Morning Herald*. Sydney Morning Herald, 16 Jan. 2011. Web. 17 Aug. 2012.

INDEX

PHOTO CREDITS

Stephen Patterson/iStockphoto, cover; Shutterstock Images, 2, 5 (top), 31, 33, 76, 79, 90, 107, 131; Debra James/Shutterstock Images, 5 (center), 39, 128 (top); Dmitriy Yakoviev/Shutterstock Images, 5 (bottom), 41; Ronald Sumners/Shutterstock Images, 6; Matt Kania/Map Hero, Inc., 9, 19, 23, 67, 109; Phillip Minnis/Shutterstock Images, 10; Andrew Dobroskok/Shutterstock Images, 13; Will Parker/Shutterstock Images, 16, 128 (bottom); Tommaso Lizzul/Shutterstock Images, 24; iStockphoto, 27, 28, 64, 68, 72, 115, 118, 121, 130, 132, 133; Alexander Chaikin/Shutterstock Images, 36; David Hyde/Shutterstock Images, 44; Bettmann/Corbis/AP Images, 46, 54, 60, 129 (top); Algernon Mayow Talmage/Getty Images, 51; Library of Congress, 58; Mark Graham/ AP Images, 63; Justin Sanson/Newspix/Rex Feat/AP Images, 75; Dmitri Ogleznev/Shutterstock Images, 84; Neale Cousland/Shutterstock Images, 87; Alex Ellinghausen/AP Images, 92; Mark Baker/AP Images, 95; Andrew Taylor/AP Images, 96, 129 (bottom); First Class Photos PTY LTD/ Shutterstock Images, 99; CPL Bernard Pearson/Australian Defense Department/AP Images, 102; Kharidehal Abhirama Ashwin/AP Images, 104; Johan Larson/Shutterstock Images, 112; John Stillwell/PA Wire/AP Images, 122; Greg Wood/Getty Images, 126